Wildflowers
Across the
Prairies

Wildflowers
Across the
Prairies

F. R. Vance
J. R. Jowsey
J. S. McLean

Western Producer Prairie Books
Saskatoon, Saskatchewan

Fenton R. Vance
James R. Jowsey
James S. McLean

Western Producer Prairie Books
Saskatoon, Saskatchewan

Second printing 1977

Canadian Cataloguing in Publication Data

Vance, Fenton R., 1907-
Wildflowers across the prairies

Bibliography:
Includes indexes.
ISBN 0-919306-74-8 bd.
ISBN 0-919306-73-X pa.
1.,Wild flowers-Prairie Provinces-
Identification. I. Jowsey, James R., 1925-
II. McLean, James S., 1940- III. Title.
QK201.V35 582'.13'09712 C77-002027-5

Cover designed by Jean MacGregor

Printed in Canada by
Modern Press
Saskatoon, Saskatchewan

To Lloyd T. Carmichael, whose earlier book, Prairie Wildflowers, *provided an introduction of wildflowers to his friends and associates in natural history, we dedicate this book.*

CONTENTS

PREFACE

Wildflowers Across the Prairies is a book for field use and for reading enjoyment by both casual and serious observers of plants. It includes one or more color illustrations and line drawings of some 270 species of the plants which are a part of the natural scene in western Canada and the adjoining "Great Plains states" of the United States of America. It is a book for all those who have known the wild plants of the prairies and their forest edges.

It is a book for beginning students (grade 4 and up) who can see plants in flower and use the illustrations to identify the plants they see. It is a book for use by high school and university students of biology whose studies may involve recognition of native plants.

This book on wildflowers is, in general, a book to "open the eyes" of people of all ages as they look at the flowers of this region of North America. It is for travellers who come here from far lands, and for those who have lived on these prairies. It is a book for farmers and summer cottage residents, for those who visit our parks, and for those who walk or drive in cities and along the roads of Saskatchewan and neighboring areas. It is a book for all students of the natural world.

Scientific names identify each plant with certainty and provide the serious student with a reliable field guide to plants of Saskatchewan and similar adjacent areas, including Manitoba, Alberta, North West Territories, Montana, the Dakotas, and Minnesota (see Figure 1). The illustrations in this book provide a useful base for plant observation throughout the whole circled area in Figure 1. Reference to "the area" in the HABITAT section on each plant refers specifically to the settled areas of Saskatchewan up to and including the edges of the boreal forest region.

Most readers will use only the common names of the plants and may wish to add other common names to the ones used here. In general, the names accepted in Canada Agriculture Publication No. 1397, *Common and Botanical Names of Weeds in Canada* (1975), are the ones used for each plant. The Canada Agriculture Publication No. 983, *Wild Plants of the Canadian Prairies* (1964), has been used extensively in verifying field observations and preparing descriptive material. Readers may wish to personally notate locations and flowering dates. Locations and flowering dates given are intended to provide the reader with a general idea of the range of these two details of the natural history of the plant involved.

While the botanical names of the plants described in this book have been thoroughly checked in several references, serious students of botany may wish to refer to other references for the descriptions of the plant species involved or the description of related plants. The general index is supplemented with an index of the plant families which are represented by the species described.

There are over 1300 species of plants described in Brietung's *Annotated Catalogue of the Vascular Flora of Saskatchewan* and the plants included in *Wildflowers Across the Prairies* are the ones which commonly appear in all or part of the area described. Introduced plants are included too if their flowers are common, and even a few plants sternly designated as "weeds," like the sow-thistle, goat's-beard, and sweet-clover, are included. There is beauty in their flowers too. Flowers of other plants will be included if a second volume of this book is prepared at a future date.

Our responsibility in the natural world is "to enjoy and not destroy." The land and its plant and animal life is a trust, not a feature to be exploited. Plants should not be picked thoughtlessly, but taken only if they are abundant. Several of the plants illustrated in this book are now very rare or may have vanished from the prairie scene. They have been indentified as rare with suitable precautions for preserving them. This is only a guide. The responsibility of each observer goes far beyond this, otherwise many more plants may vanish from the prairies. Take care! Encourage preservation of habitat for native plants. Know which species are abundant. Enjoy the flowers as they live, that succeeding generations may do the same.

Wildflowers Across the Prairies has been produced by combining the thoughts of many people, in response to frequent expressions of the need for such a book. The authors recognize that such a work would not have been possible without the financial, scientific and other assistance they received. Detailed acknowledgments are included in the section which follows, and on the "photo credits" page. The main photographic responsibilities have rested with F. R. Vance, the artistic representations of flowers by sketches were the total responsibility of J. S. McLean, and the responsibility for biological accuracy, preparation of the written descriptions of plants, assembly of the manuscript and general management of the project was borne by J. R. Jowsey.

J. R. Jowsey
February, 1977

ACKNOWLEDGMENTS

The authors acknowledge with profound gratitude the many forms of assistance provided to the Prairie Wildflowers Project and the preparation of material for this book. While such a work may have been carried on as an activity of only the authors, the assistance, material and otherwise, rendered in its preparation by many persons and organizations, has made it the work of a community of persons interested in properly identifying some of the flowers of the "northern Great Plains." It is our pleasure to acknowledge these elements of assistance as follows:

The financial support of the Canada Council with an Explorations Program grant to J. R. Jowsey used in financing the field work through which we obtained photographic material, plant specimens for sketches and plants for the development of a reference herbarium;

The support of persons who wrote on behalf of the application of J. R. Jowsey for the grant to be received under the Canada Council Explorations Program, namely Dr. G. F. Ledingham, Dr. W. A. Quick and Dr. M. Evelyn Jonescu of the Departments of Biology and Secondary Education of the University of Regina;

The extended period of assistance of K. F. Best, Canada Agriculture Research Station, Regina, through the designing of the project, confirmation of identification of specimens and the checking of the manuscript for botanical accuracy and form;

The assistance and patience of all those who submitted slides for consideration for this book. Inclusion of slides taken by persons other than the authors has at once speeded the completion of this project and has expanded the feeling of community within the group of persons involved. (Those persons who contributed one or more color slides are listed on the last page of this book, under "Photo Credits");

The role of Shirley Jowsey in the development of the design of this book on wildflowers, in typing of the numerous stages of the manuscript, in the receipt and cataloguing of slides, sketches and plants in our reference herbarium, and in management of the details of the project in its various stages.

INTRODUCTION

Wildflowers Across the Prairies includes descriptions of some 270 species of flowering plants of the northern tip of the "Great Plains of North America" (Figure 1). Most species are described by two color pictures: one of the flower or group of flowers, the other of a whole plant or a group of plants in their natural habitat. A sketch and a brief description of FLOWERS, FRUIT, LEAVES, GROWTH HABIT and HABITAT is also included. In the interests of accurate comparison of plants, some pages differ through the introduction of another color illustration of a similar plant of the same genus, or through replacement of the sketch with a color illustration of the fruit of the species involved. The order in which plants are arranged in this book is the traditional taxonomic order followed by botanists and others who study plants. Within plant families, the next taxonomic division, genus, has an alphabetic arrangement, as does the arrangement of species within each genus. For the general reader use of the index will locate any plant by either common name or genus.

In a few cases, plants of different genera are included on the same page. For instance, on page 145, three plants of different genera are included: the large white ground-cherry, wild tomato and black henbane. They are shown on the same page to establish a clear comparison of these three poisonous members of the potato family (Solanacae). Another page, (109), which departs significantly from the usual arrangement includes two sketches of plants commonly confused; the water-hemlock, (*Cicuta* spp.), and the water-parsnip, (*Sium* spp.). The two sketches clearly illustrate differences in the leaves and in the inflorescence of the plants involved, and a single color picture shows the water-hemlock in its natural habitat.

The line drawings or sketches used are intended to draw attention to a particular feature of the plant involved. In some cases they are magnified several times to show such features, and this should be noted if any distortion of the plant is apparent at first examination of the sketch. All sketches are based on use of fresh specimens, usually observed under field conditions, but references to a herbarium maintained for the purpose, and to other herbaria in Regina supplemented the observation of the artist (JSM) in the field.

The description of terms in the glossary which follows this introduction has been supplemented by several figures. Figure 1 presents the major concentration of the plants of the 270 species described in this book. Figures 2 through 8 are intended to provide the reader with a visual impression of such terms as *pinnate,* in the case of leaves, *corymb,* in the case of flowers, etc. These figures are reproduced from Budd and Best's *Wild Plants of the Canadian Prairies.* Since they were originally sketched by the late Arch. C. Budd, it is with particular pleasure that the authors use them in *Wildflowers Across the Prairies.*

2

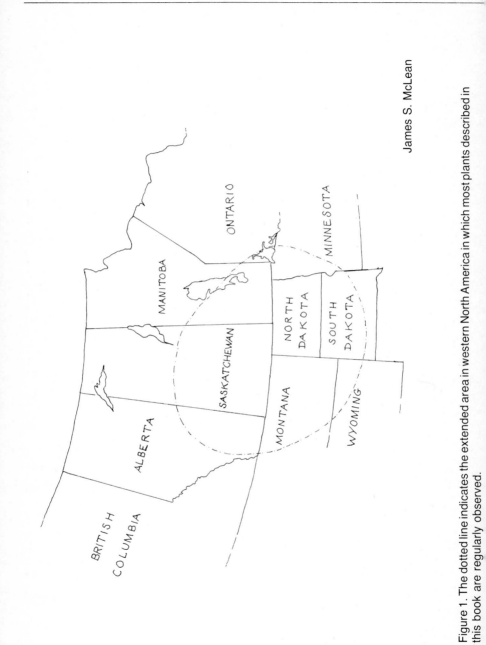

James S. McLean

Figure 1. The dotted line indicates the extended area in western North America in which most plants described in this book are regularly observed.

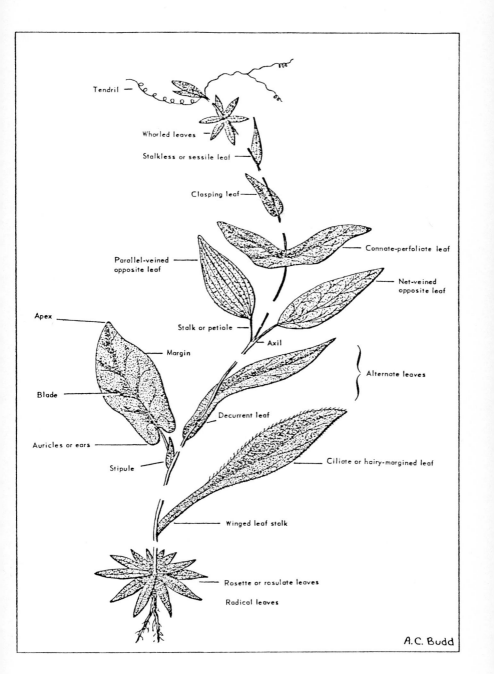

Figure 2. Leaf variations.

4

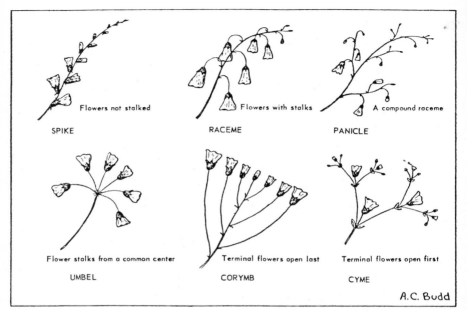

Figure 3. Types of inflorescence.

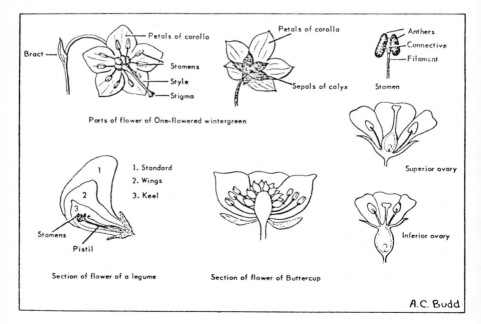

Figure 4. Flower parts.

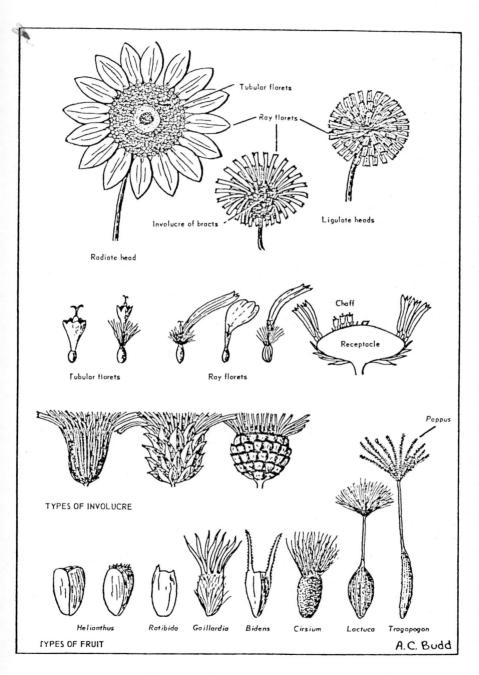

Figure 5. Characteristics of composite flowers and fruits.

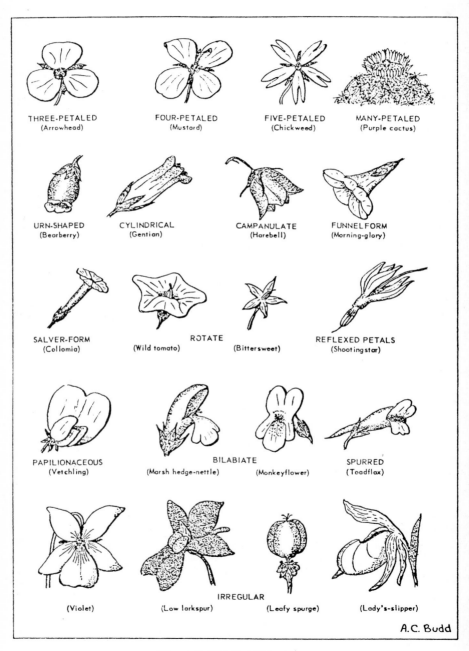

THREE-PETALED
(Arrowhead)

FOUR-PETALED
(Mustard)

FIVE-PETALED
(Chickweed)

MANY-PETALED
(Purple cactus)

URN-SHAPED
(Bearberry)

CYLINDRICAL
(Gentian)

CAMPANULATE
(Harebell)

FUNNELFORM
(Morning-glory)

SALVER-FORM
(Collomia)

ROTATE
(Wild tomato)

(Bittersweet)

REFLEXED PETALS
(Shooting star)

PAPILIONACEOUS
(Vetchling)

BILABIATE
(Marsh hedge-nettle)

(Monkeyflower)

SPURRED
(Toadflax)

IRREGULAR

(Violet)

(Low larkspur)

(Leafy spurge)

(Lady's-slipper)

A.C. Budd

Figure 6. Types of flowers.

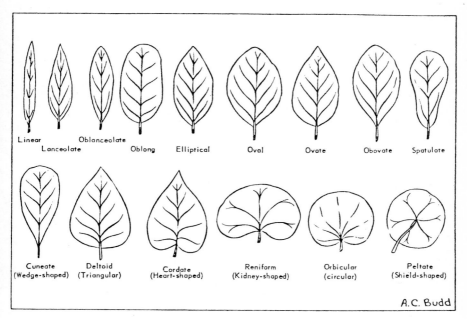

Figure 7. Shapes of simple leaves.

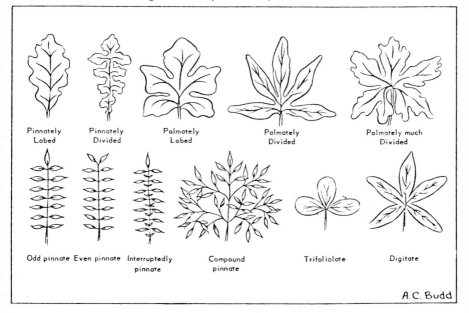

Figure 8. Types of divided leaves.

CATTAIL
Typha latifolia L.

Cattail   early flowering stage

FLOWERS are minute, brown and lack sepals and petals. They are arranged in a familiar dense cylindrical spike which is 3 to 6 inches (7.5-15 cm) long and about an inch (2.5 cm) in diameter. The pale green upper portion of the spike carries the male flowers and disappears, usually due to being broken off. The thicker brown section holds the female flowers. Flowers appear in July. The FRUIT is a minute, tufted achene which bears one seed. LEAVES are light olive green, parallel-veined, 10 to 20 inches (25-50 cm) in length, with a long sheath to the base of the flowering stalk. GROWTH HABIT is perennial from thick creeping roots. The flower stalk acts as the core of the plant and is surrounded by the basal leaves. The flower stem may be ¼ inch (6 mm) thick and a total height 3 to 5 feet (1-2.5 m). HABITAT includes the deeper sloughs and marshes or roadside ditches, beyond the range of sedges and bulrushes, where water persists until at least midsummer.

Cattail

ARROWHEAD
Sagittaria cuneata Sheld.

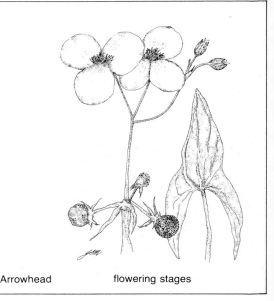

Arrowhead   flowering stages

FLOWERS (staminate and pistillate types on the same plant) are waxy white and have three petals. There is a conspicuous yellow center in the male flowers which are usually borne higher on the flowering stalk than the female flowers. Blooms are usually in whorls of three, appearing July-August. FRUITS are flattened achenes which develop from the carpels, (three to four) of the female flowers. They are arranged in a dense head. LEAVES are broad and arrow-shaped, entire margined, deep green above and lighter below. There are usually a few narrow, strap-shaped underwater leaves. Aerial leaves may be 4 inches (10 cm) long and 1½ inches (4 cm) wide. GROWTH HABIT is perennial; height may be 8 to 16 inches (20-40 cm), depending to some extent on the depth of water where the plant grows. HABITAT includes shallow sloughs, the semi-open areas of marshes, roadside ditches, etc., throughout the area.

Arrowhead

WATER CALLA
Calla palustris L.

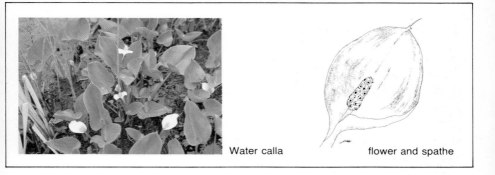

Water calla   flower and spathe

FLOWERS are minute, yellowish, and lack sepals and petals. They develop in a thick spike-like spadix which is backed by a white oval spathe that is 1 to 1½ inches (2.5-4 cm) long. The modified flower stem (scape) may be up to 4 inches (10 cm) long. Flowers appear June-July. FRUIT is a red berry formed in a dense fleshy head. The white spathe rots away as the fruit develops. LEAVES are basal, broadly ovate, parallel veined, 2 to 4 inches (5-10 cm) long, on stalks of varying length, 2 to 8 inches (5-20 cm). GROWTH HABIT is perennial from thick rhizomes that root at the nodes. Total height is 4 to 8 inches (10-20 cm) but some of this is under water so plants appear shorter. HABITAT includes boggy sloughs and ditches where water remains well into August, particularly in the northern and eastern parts of the area. This plant is occasionally referred to as water-arum.

Water calla

NODDING ONION
Allium cernuum Roth

Nodding onion

Pink-flowered onion

FLOWERS are pinkish lavender to white, eight to twelve in a loose nodding cluster at the end of a slender stem. Each flower is, like other onions, lily shaped, about ¼ inch (6 mm) long, with the two outer floral rings combined into six similar petals. Flowers of the pink-flowered onion, (*A. stellatum* Fraser), are similar but erect in the inflorescence, appearing June-August. FRUIT is a dry capsule, developing from the three-loculed ovary. LEAVES are fairly numerous, narrow, medium green, circular but not hollow. GROWTH HABIT is erect and the leaves and the single flower cluster arise from a rather small, coarse-necked bulb. The flower stalks are nodding when blooms are present but become erect before seeds mature. Length of the flower stalk varies from 4 to 16 inches (10-40 cm). HABITAT commonly includes open prairie and edges of scrubby patches. It is widely distributed in the same type of habitat as the prairie onion but is not as common. The pink-flowered onion is more common in the eastern and northern parts of the area.

Nodding onion

PRAIRIE ONION
Allium textile Nels. and Macbr.

Prairie onion

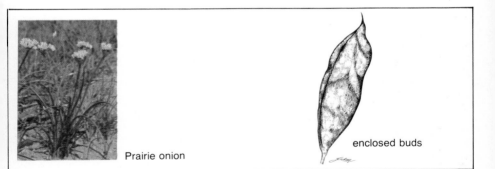

Prairie onion

enclosed buds

FLOWERS are white, occasionally tinged with pink, with the color due to similar petals and sepals (three each). They are borne in several rather tight umbels on stems which arise from the bulb, and appear May-June. FRUIT is a small, dry capsule containing four to six seeds. LEAVES are narrow, grooved and circular, characteristic of the onion family, complete with a strong odor and taste. They are not strictly hollow as are cultivated onions and wild chives, (*A. schoenoprasum* L. var. *sibiricum* [L.] Hartm.). GROWTH HABIT is erect, with several grass-like stems (leaves) arising from a bulb about ⅜ to ½ inch (10-12 mm) diameter. Height, 3 to 10 inches (7-30 cm), is usually less than that of other native onions. HABITAT commonly includes the dry prairie meadows and hillsides in the southern third of the area. It is probably the most widely distributed of the native onions.

FAIRYBELLS
Disporum trachycarpum (S. Wats.) B. and H.

Fairybells

Fairybells

Fairybells

FLOWERS are greenish yellow to white, ½ to ¾ inch (12-20 mm) long, with the petals and sepals forming a single floral ring of six segments. From one to four blooms grow together like miniature lilies on drooping stalks among the leaves, appearing in June. FRUIT is a velvety-surfaced berry which goes through an orange stage and is red when completely ripe. The berry is ¼ to ⅝ inch (6-15 mm) diameter, soft and filled with small seeds. LEAVES are bright green, broadly ovate to lance-shaped, stalkless, parallel-veined, up to 3 inches (7.5 cm) long, and 2 inches (5 cm) wide. GROWTH HABIT is perennial, with many drooping leafy branches, 8 to 24 inches (20-60 cm) tall, usually nearer 8 inches (20 cm). Plants grow from a prominent horizontal rhizome. HABITAT includes moist wooded areas, thickets — saskatoon, chokecherry, etc., usually in association with sarsaparilla and baneberry. It is well distributed through the central part, (Qu'-Appelle Valley and its tributaries), and the east and north edges of the area.

WESTERN RED LILY
Lilium philadelphicum L. var. *andinum* (Nutt.) Ker.

Western red lily

Western red lily   root and bulblets

This is Saskatchewan's floral emblem. FLOWERS are bright red, with bases of petals more orange than red and dotted with black, 2½ inches (7 cm) long and up to 3 inches (7.5 cm) across, with single or multiple blooms. Sepals and petals are both colored. Flowers appear in June. FRUIT is an elongated egg-shaped capsule in three sections. The LEAVES, linear to lance-shaped, alternate on stem with upper leaves in a whorl at the base of the flower stalk. The wood lily has all leaves in whorls. GROWTH HABIT is erect, perennial from a clump of white bulblets, usually 8-24 inches (20-60 cm) tall. Common HABITAT includes moist meadows, edges of aspen groves, thickets, and roadside ditches throughout the area.

FALSE SOLOMON'S-SEAL
Smilacina stellata (L.) Desf.

False solomon's-seal

False solomon's-seal

FLOWERS are small, up to ¼ inch (6 mm) in diameter, borne in a loose spike-like raceme at the end of a leafy stem. The three petals and the three sepals are white and 1/16 to ⅛ inch (3-5 mm) long. Flowers appear in early May. FRUIT is a greenish berry with brownish black stripes. LEAVES are opposite, light green, smooth above and slightly hairy underneath, from 1 to 5 inches (2.5-12 cm) long, often folded along the midrib. GROWTH HABIT is perennial, erect but on bent stems about 6 to 8 inches (15-20 cm) long and occasionally up to 18 inches (45 cm). A larger species, wild spikenard, (*S. racemosa* [L.] Desf.), has similar flowers but the berries are red when ripe. HABITAT includes moist woods, shores of sandy marshes and margins of scrubby patches. A similar plant often growing in the same habitat is *Maianthemum canadense* Desf. var. *interius* Fern., known as two-leaved solomon's-seal or wild lily-of-the-valley. Its height is usually under 6 inches (15 cm). It is different due to its two or three leaves and red berries.

Wild spikenard

CARRIONFLOWER
Smilax herbacea L. var. *lasioneura* (Hook.) A. DC.

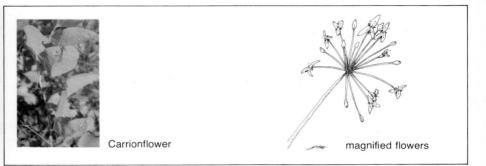

Carrionflower   magnified flowers

FLOWERS are greenish white, small 3/32 inch or 2 mm diameter) in an umbel of twenty to forty flowers. The name of the plant comes from the carrion-like odor of the flowers. This is probably an evolutionary adaptation to attract flies which aid in fertilization. Approximate flowering date is June. FRUIT is a bluish black berry about 3/16 inch (4 mm) diameter, with a light bloom. There are usually four to six seeds per fruit. LEAVES are alternate, light green and have some netting in the arrangement of the veins. The dominant veins are parallel, as in other monocotyledons. Each leaf is 1½ to 5 inches (4-12 cm) long on petioles ½ to 2½ inches (1-7 cm) long, oval, pointed at the apex and rounded at the base. GROWTH HABIT: A climbing shrub with a weak stem and long tendrils, which attains a length of 4 to 6 feet (1.5-2m). The stems are woody but die back each year. HABITAT includes the shady moist areas of scrub, open woods and river valleys in the central and eastern part of the area.

Carrionflower

SMOOTH CAMAS
Zygadenus elegans Pursh

Smooth camas

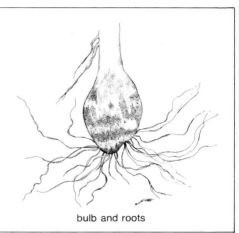

bulb and roots

Smooth camas

FLOWERS are yellowish white or greenish white and lily-shaped in an open raceme. The inner edges of the base petals and sepals (similar) are powdery yellow. They are about ⅜ inch (10 mm) long and ½ inch (12 mm) in diameter, appearing in June. FRUIT is a three-lobed, many seeded capsule, egg-shaped and ¾ inch (2 cm) long. LEAVES are pale green, mainly basal, 4 to 8 inches (10-20 cm) long, linear, keeled and almost grass-like, 1/16 inch (2 mm) wide. GROWTH HABIT is tall, 1 to 2 feet (30-60 cm) with a lily-like appearance. It is taller than death camas, *(Z. gramineus* Rydb.), and the inflorescence is much longer. HABITAT includes the moist, more saline areas of meadows and roadsides of the parkland and prairie, and scrubby areas, particularly in the east and central parts of the area. Death camas is found only in the southwest part of the area.

DEATH CAMAS
Zygadenus gramineus Rydb.

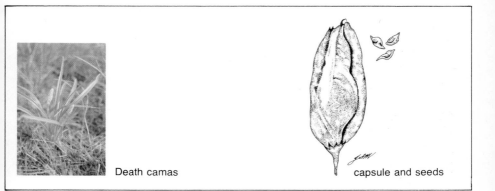

Death camas

capsule and seeds

FLOWERS are pale yellow, 3/16 inch (4 mm) long and about the same in diameter, tubular in profile. They are arranged in a dense raceme at the ends of the stems. Flowers appear May-June. The FRUIT is an oblong many-seeded capsule. LEAVES are pale green, linear, sheathed at the base, 4 to 8 inches (10-20 cm) long and about ⅛ inch (3 mm) wide. GROWTH HABIT is grass-like, 4 to 8 inches (10-20 cm), from a deep bulb. It begins growth early in the spring. This increases its hazard to ranchers because it is particularly poisonous to sheep and somewhat poisonous to cattle. HABITAT includes the higher edges of slough margins and draws and coulees of the southwest.

Death camas

BLUE-EYED GRASS
Sisyrinchium montanum Greene

Blue-eyed grass

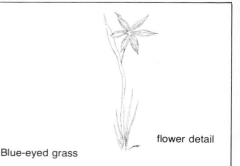

flower detail

Blue-eyed grass

FLOWERS are bright blue, ¼ inch (6 mm) diameter, with three petals and three sepals. They are distinctly star-shaped and appear June-July. FRUIT is a ¼ inch (6 mm) long, globular capsule, in three sections, containing small black seeds. LEAVES are bright green, linear and grass-like, basal with winged margins and usually ⅛ inch (3 mm) wide. GROWTH HABIT is erect, 3 to 12 inches (7-30 cm) high, often in colonies among grasses. A smaller, tufted species, *S. mucronatum* Michx., has lighter blue flowers and is more common in saline areas. HABITAT includes relatively moist areas, with the species difference in tolerance of salinity noted above. Blue-eyed grass will grow from naturally fallen seed in any reasonably moist sandy soil.

VENUS-SLIPPER
Calypso bulbosa (L.) Oakes

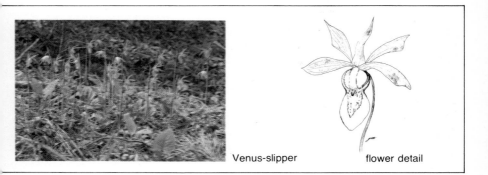

Venus-slipper   flower detail

FLOWERS are pale purple to pink with the typical orchid arrangement of sepals and petals. The whole flower is ½ to 1 inch (12-25 mm) long. The pink sac-like lip has darker purple lines on it and is more striking due to an inner tuft of yellow hairs. Flowers appear in early June. FRUIT is a brown capsule, ½ inch (12 mm) long, containing many seeds. LEAVES are dark green, one per plant, basal, wide ovate 1 to 1½ inches (2.5-4 cm) long. GROWTH HABIT is short, with the flower on a 3 to 7 inch (7-17 cm) stem. The stem is slender and the flowers may appear nearly prostrate. HABITAT is open coniferous woods, particularly under pine. This orchid, named "Calypso" for the Greek goddess of that name, favors the open shaded areas in the northern forest.

Venus-slipper

SPOTTED CORALROOT
Corallorhiza maculata Raf.

Spotted coralroot   flower detail

FLOWERS are light pink to white, liberally spotted with purple or red on sepals and petals. They are 3/16 to ⅝ inch (4-14 mm) long, with the lip, which is also spotted, about the same length. Blooms have a prominent yellowish spur. Ten to forty of them are borne in a long raceme, appearing May-June. FRUIT is a round many-seeded capsule. LEAVES are reduced to scales about ⅛ inch (3 mm) wide and an inch (2.5 cm) or more long, dark reddish brown in color. GROWTH HABIT is erect and saprophytic. They are 6 to 20 inches (15-50 cm) tall, with at least half of this height due to the raceme. HABITAT is the forest floor in deep coniferous woods. It is found on the edges of the mixed forest and in the Cypress Hills.

Spotted coralroot

STRIPED CORALROOT
Corallorhiza striata Lindl.

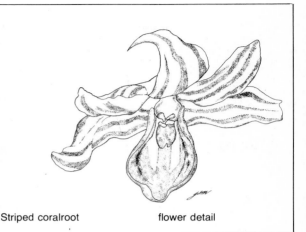

Striped coralroot   flower detail

FLOWERS are lavender pink with dark reddish purple stripes in the lateral petals and sepals. The lip is white to light pink with five purple stripes. The flowers are about ½ inch (12 mm) long, spurless, in a raceme of fewer blooms, (10-25), than the spotted coralroot, *(C. maculata* Raf.). Approximate flowering dates range from May-June. FRUIT is a round, many-seeded capsule about 3/16 inch (4 mm) in diameter. LEAVES are reduced to long, colorless, scale-like structures which sheath the stem. GROWTH HABIT is erect and saprophytic. The coarse, stout, reddish to yellowish stems may reach a total height of 18 to 20 inches (45-50 cm) of which at least one-third is due to the flowering stalk. On average, these plants are shorter than those of spotted coralroot. HABITAT is the same for both species: deep coniferous woods. They are often found in the same area, at the boreal forest edge, and in the Cypress Hills.

Striped coralroot

STEMLESS LADY'S SLIPPER
Cypripedium acaule Ait.

Stemless lady's slipper

This is the floral emblem of Prince Edward Island. FLOWERS are dominated by a pink lip, 2 to 2½ inches (5-7 cm) long, deeply cleft near its center. Sepals and petals are lanceolate, yellow green to greenish brown. Flowers are solitary and the flowering stem is leafless and hairy. It grows from the root crown. Flowering occurs in late June. FRUIT is a brown, many-seeded capsule. LEAVES are basal, medium green, and there are only two, nearly opposite in placement. They are narrowly elliptic or oblong and sparsely hairy, about 6 inches (15 cm) long. GROWTH HABIT is erect, 6 to 15 inches (15-40 cm) tall with leaves and stems arising from coarse roots. Common HABITAT includes bogs and other moist areas among sand dunes in the open shade in northern forest areas. These flowers are rare — do not pick!

Stemless lady's slipper

RAM'S HEAD LADY'S SLIPPER
Cypripedium arietinum R. Br.

Ram's head lady's slipper

Ram's head lady's slipper

Franklin's lady's slipper

FLOWERS are greenish purple, solitary, with sepals and lateral petals ½ to 1 inch (12-24 mm) long. The lip is whitish with heavy purplish veins, ½ to ¾ inch (1-2 cm) long and ends in a spur-like horn. The other lady's slipper illustration is *C. passerinum* Richards., known by various common names: northern lady's slipper, sparrows egg lady's slipper and Franklin's lady's slipper. Generally, flowers appear in June. FRUIT is a brown capsule charac-teristic of the lady's slippers. LEAVES, three to five, are dark green and lance-shaped to elliptic. They are often folded and have marginal hairs. GROWTH HABIT is erect and slender, 4 to 15 inches (10-40 cm) high, usually nearer the former. Common HABITAT includes damp, cool sandy areas in woodlands in the north and north-east. This plant is very rare in Saskatch-ewan. Sites where it still grows should be carefully preserved.

LARGE YELLOW LADY'S SLIPPER
Cypripedium calceolus L. var. *pubescens* (Willd.) Correll

flower detail

Large yellow lady's slipper

Large yellow lady's slipper

FLOWERS are bright yellow with sepals and petals greenish to brown. The lip may be ¾ to 1½ inches (2-4 cm) long and may have a few brown or reddish purple spots near the tongue. Flowers appear in June. FRUIT is a dry, dark brown capsule with many seeds. LEAVES are light green, ovate to lanceolate with sharp points, prominently veined and with a few hairs. They are 2 to 6 inches (5-15 cm) long and up to 2 inches (5 cm) wide. GROWTH HABIT is perennial, flower stem is usually about 5 inches (12 cm) long and nearly smooth. The total plant varies in height from 6 to 16 inches (15-40 cm). HABITAT includes the edges or open spaces in aspen poplar woods or upper margins of sloughs and ditches on roads and railway grades. Both this variety and the small yellow lady's slipper, (*C. calceolus* [L.] var. *parviflorum* [Salisb.] Fern.), are rare and should only be picked or moved under special restrictions or permit.

SHOWY LADY'S SLIPPER
Cypripedium reginae Walt.

Showy lady's slipper

FLOWERS have a light pink lip with reddish purple stripes; otherwise, sepals and petals are white. The lip is often over an inch (2.5 cm) long and the total flower may be 1½ inches (4 cm) in length, blooming June-July. FRUIT is a somewhat elongated, round, many-seeded capsule to which the dried flower may be attached for many weeks. LEAVES are opposite, light green, and hairy, particularly on the underside. They are fairly numerous and each one clasps the stem over a distance of several inches. LEAVES are about 1½ inches (4 cm) across and length varies from 4 to 8 inches (10-20 cm). GROWTH HABIT is erect and perennial on rather thick hairy stems well covered with leaves. Plants are tall, usually about 15 inches (37 cm) but 2 to 2½ feet (60-75 cm) is not unusual. HABITAT includes the open shade in low spruce and pine stands, where the soil is calcareous, particularly on high calcium, low magnesium soils. This plant is relatively common in Manitoba but is rare in Saskatchewan, and may have been eliminated here. Take care!

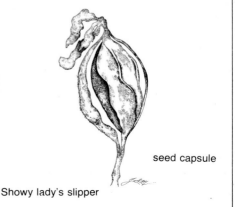

Showy lady's slipper

seed capsule

ROUND-LEAVED ORCHIS
Orchis rotundifolia Banks

Round-leaved orchis

Round-leaved orchis

Round-leaved bog-orchid

FLOWERS are rose pink to white, ⅜ to ¾ inch (1-2 cm) long in a bracted raceme of two to eight flowers, with color mainly due to lateral petals. The lip is white with purple spots, about ⅜ inch (1 cm) long, three-lobed, with the middle lobe the largest and notched at the apex. The spur is slender, curved and much shorter than the lip. The lateral petals spread outwards and the upper sepal and petals are elevated above the lip. Flowers are greenish white in the round-leaved bog-orchid, (*Habenaria orbiculata* [Pursh] Torr.). Flowers bloom in July. FRUIT is a dry, brown, many-seeded capsule. LEAVES: This species has only one leaf. The round-leaved bog-orchid has two rounded leaves and its flower stalk is much longer. Leaves are basal in both species. GROWTH HABIT is basal, with a long, stiff flower stalk which may be 4 to 10 inches (10-25 cm) high. The leaf and flower stem arise from a scaly rootstock. HABITAT includes the boreal forest and its parkland edges, where moisture conditions are good. This plant and the *Habenaria* species described are fairly common in this habitat.

HOODED LADY'S-TRESSES
Spiranthes romanzoffiana Cham.

Nodding lady's-tresses

FLOWERS are sweet scented, creamy white, about ¼ inch (6 mm) long, each on a short stalk in three spirals on a spike 1 to 3 inches (3-8 cm) long. The hood is formed of three sepals and two lateral petals, and in profile looks like the brim of a sunbonnet. The lip is fiddle-shaped, spurless, about ⅜ inch (1 cm) long and bent abruptly downward. Flower arrangement is more open on the other plant illustrated which is nodding lady's tresses, sometimes considered a separate species, *S. cernua* Rich. Blooms appear July-August. FRUIT is a small capsule which contains many seeds. LEAVES are linear to lanceolate, 2 to 6 inches (5-15 cm) long, blunt-tipped and extending along the stem rather than basal as is the case with slender lady's tresses, *(S. gracilis* [Bigel.] Beck.). GROWTH HABIT is perennial and erect, on rather stout stems, usually short but occasionally over 12 inches (30 cm) tall. HABITAT includes swampy places, meadows and open woods with light shade, lake shores, boreal and parkland areas, particularly in the north and east.

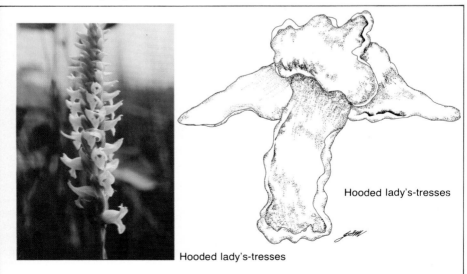

Hooded lady's-tresses

Hooded lady's-tresses

COMMON HOP

Humulus lupulus L.

Common hop

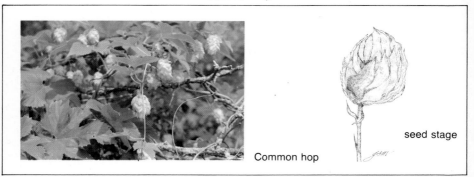

Common hop

seed stage

FLOWERS of different sexes are on different plants, (i.e., hop is dioecious.) Male flowers are green, small, in loose panicles in leaf axils, each with five sepals and five stamens. Female flowers have the calyx reduced to a single sepal. They are in drooping catkin-like spikes and are located in the leaf axils. Approximate flowering date is June. FRUIT is a resinous achene, covered with scaly, sharp, modified bracts. These clusters of bracts may be a ½ inch (12 mm) across and more than an inch (2.5 cm) long. LEAVES are numerous, opposite, light green, palmately lobed into three to seven leaflets. The upper leaves are often toothed rather than divided. The whole leaf may be 4 to 7 inches (10-18 cm) wide and has whitish or yellowish glandular spots on the underside. GROWTH HABIT is perennial. The stems are woody but usually die back each season. They twine over shrubs and may reach 20 feet (6 m) in length. HABITAT includes moist places in wooded areas, roadside ditches, etc., particularly in the Qu'Appelle Valley and tributaries, and in the eastern part of the area generally.

PALE COMANDRA
Comandra pallida A. DC.

Pale comandra   flower detail

FLOWERS are greenish white to pink, ⅛ to ³/₁₆ inch (3-5 mm) in length, and about ³/₁₆ inch (5 mm) across with five petals and five sepals. They are borne in clusters of three to five at the tips of stems, blooming May-June. FRUIT is a hard, olive green drupe with one seed. LEAVES are alternate, pale gray green, linear-lanceolate, ½ to 1 inch (1-2.5 cm) long, smooth, and usually lacking petioles. They are numerous and cause the plant to appear very leafy. GROWTH HABIT is erect and perennial, with many stems often arising from one point on the creeping rootstock. Plants are usually 3 to 5 inches (7-12 cm) tall but may be over 12 inches (30 cm). HABITAT includes dry sandy hillsides throughout the whole area, particularly on the open prairie.

Pale comandra

YELLOW UMBRELLAPLANT
Eriogonum flavum Nutt.

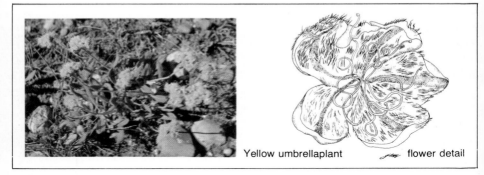

Yellow umbrellaplant   flower detail

FLOWERS are pale yellow with a tinge of orange. Petals are absent and the floral ring is formed of united sepals. Flowers are borne in fluffy clusters, about ½ inch (12 mm) diameter, which are encased with several large leaf-like bracts. Approximate flowering date is June. The FRUIT is a small, ⅛ inch (3 mm) achene, with soft matted hairs. LEAVES are basal, green above, white on the underside due to fine hairs, 1¼ to 2 inches (3-5 cm) long, linear-oblong or spatulate. GROWTH HABIT is perennial and erect, from a coarse, woody, tufted root. It is characteristically a low plant, usually 4 to 8 inches (10-20 cm) but may be as tall as 16 inches (40 cm). HABITAT includes dry eroded areas, hillsides, badland exposures and canyon walls throughout the southwest.

Yellow umbrellaplant

WATER SMARTWEED
Polygonum amphibium L.

Water smartweed

Swamp smartweed

Lady's thumb

FLOWERS are reddish purple, about ¹/₁₆ inch (2 mm) in diameter, in dense spikes. The color is due to the five sepals. Petals are absent. Flowers bloom July-August. FRUIT is a small lens-shaped achene, which contains a black seed. It is a common food for ducks. LEAVES are lanceolate to ovate, 4 to 8 inches (10-20 cm) long, deep green and hairless above, often hairy beneath. A few of the lower leaves may be floating. GROWTH HABIT is perennial and more or less erect. Stems are angled and wiry but weak. Height may be up to 15 inches (38 cm) and some plants float on their stems. Swamp smartweed or persicaria, *(P. coccineum* Muhl.), also shown here, tends to have stronger stems and grow taller. The third illustration is lady's thumb, *(P. persicaria* L.), a shorter (4 to 6 inches or 10-15 cm) species. HABITAT includes shallow sloughs, slough margins and drainage ditches in the prairie and parkland. Smartweed turns whole sloughs rose pink in July of some years. The swamp species and lady's-thumb take over in slightly drier terrain in marshes.

WESTERN DOCK
Rumex occidentalis S. Wats.

Western dock

Western dock

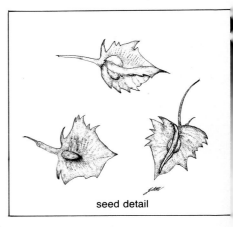

seed detail

FLOWERS are greenish, extremely small (under 1 mm), and densely packed in a small cluster. There are six sepals but no petals and three of the sepals are much larger than the others. Blooms appear June-July. The FRUIT is a three-sided achene enclosed in the dry papery reddish brown sepals. This gives the plants their characteristic appearance in late summer. Examination of the fruit with a microscope is about the only sure way to separate some of the species of dock. LEAVES are alternate, bright green, simple, oblong to lanceolate, thick and heart-shaped at the base. They may be up to 12 inches (30 cm) long and the lower leaves are much larger than the upper ones. GROWTH HABIT is perennial, tall, to 3 feet (1 m) or more in some cases, with a reddish stem arising from a woody taproot. Leaves are rather sparse and the plant is most noticed by its inflorescence. This may be over a foot (30 cm) long, and dark reddish brown when ripe. Other similar species are the field docks, *(R. fennicus* [Murb.]), and *(R. stenophyllus* [Ledeb.]). HABITAT includes sloughs and roadside ditches, etc. throughout the area. Field dock and narrow-leaved dock tend to be more common than western dock in similar niches in more northerly, central and eastern parts of the area.

SPRINGBEAUTY
Claytonia lanceolata Pursh

Springbeauty

flower detail

FLOWERS are white, occasionally with pink lines or shading on the five petals, star-shaped, about ½ inch (12 mm) across. There are only two sepals. Several blooms are borne in a loose raceme. Flowering occurs in May. FRUIT is a papery capsule about ⅛ inch (3 mm) long which contains many small black seeds. LEAVES are shiny dark green, lanceolate, ¾ to 1½ inches (2-4 cm) long, and stalkless. Occasionally plants have one or two stalked basal leaves and there are usually only two stem leaves. GROWTH HABIT is low but not exactly prostrate, growing from a ¾ inch (2 cm) corm found about 3 inches (8 cm) below ground. The reddish stems are short but may elevate plants 2 inches (5 cm) or more in a mat of dark green leaves. HABITAT commonly includes the shallow draws and south-facing slopes of the southwest. It is rare but still found in some places in the Cypress Hills.

Springbeauty

FIELD CHICKWEED
Cerastium arvense L.

Field chickweed   flower detail

Mouse-eared chickweed

FLOWERS are white, ⅜ to ⅝ inch (10-15 mm) across, with five deeply cleft petals and five sepals. Sepals are much shorter than petals in this species, but about the same length as the petals in another common species, mouse-eared chickweed, (*C. vulgatum* L.). Flowers bloom in May. FRUIT is a capsule about ½ inch (12 mm) long which contains several reddish brown seeds. LEAVES are opposite, linear to lanceolate, ⅜ to 1½ inch (1-4 cm) long, usually hairy and consequently gray green in color. Leaves of the mouse-eared chickweed are slightly shorter and more hairy.

GROWTH HABIT is perennial and tufted, (but mouse-eared chickweed may appear as one to four distinctly separate stems). The stems are usually semi-prostrate, 6 to 10 inches (15-25 cm) long, covered with short hairs which point downward toward the base of the plant. HABITAT includes the open prairie throughout the western and central part of the area. Field chickweed and mouse-eared chickweed differ little and often grow in the same locality. The latter is more common in and near sparse stands of aspen poplar in the north and east.

NIGHT-FLOWERING CATCHFLY
Silene noctiflora L.

Night-flowering catchfly

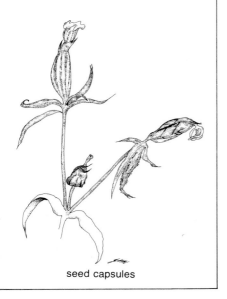

seed capsules

Cow cockle

FLOWERS are white, occasionally pale pink, up to ¾ inch (2 cm) across. They are single but the plant's branching often gives the impression of a number of flowers. Sepals are united to form a sticky, oval, tubular calyx which is ½ to ¾ inch (12-20 mm) long, striped white and dark green. Each of the five petals is deeply cleft. Range of flowering dates includes June-August. FRUIT is an ovate capsule enclosed by the calyx. The small black seeds rattle about in the capsule when mature. LEAVES are opposite, dark green, oval to lance-shaped, sticky and hairy. The upper ones are stalkless, 1 to 3 inches (2.5-7 cm) long. Basal leaves have short stalks and are 2 to 5 inches (5-12 cm) long. GROWTH HABIT is erect and branched, an annual with a coarse sticky-hairy stem, usually 15 to 36 inches (38-90 cm) tall. HABITAT includes gardens, roadside ditches, and field edges. It is a persistent, introduced weed, particularly common under good moisture conditions in the south and central parts of the area. Cow cockle, (*Saponaria vaccaria* L.), is common in the same type of habitat. It has bluish pink flowers, smooth leaves and a hairless stem.

BANEBERRY
Actaea rubra (Ait.) Willd.

Baneberry

Baneberry   flower cluster

FLOWERS are white, ⅛ inch (3 mm) across. There are four to ten white petals and three to five petal-like sepals, which fall off soon after the flower opens. The flowers are numerous, borne in a cone-shaped cluster at the end of a slender stem, and bloom in June. FRUIT is a berry ¼ to ⅜ inch (6-10 mm) in diameter, which is red in some plants and white in others. The white form is not a separate species or sub-species. These fruits are poisonous and their bright color makes them a substantial hazard where small children are involved. LEAVES are dark green and compound, with several oval, sharply toothed leaflets. They are hairy along the veins on the underside. A whole leaf may be 3 to 5 inches (7.5-12 cm) wide. GROWTH HABIT is erect and perennial; plants are usually at least 8 inches (20 cm) tall and may be over 30 inches (80 cm). HABITAT includes the moist floor of mixed forests and aspen poplar bluffs as well as the wooded ravines of the open plains. It is reasonably common throughout the area.

CANADA ANEMONE
Anemone canadensis L.

Canada anemone

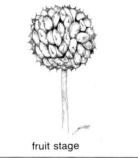

fruit stage

FLOWERS are white, 1 to 1¼ inches (2.5-3 cm) across, due to petal-like sepals; petals are lacking. Several separate flowering stems arise from the main flowering stem at a whorl of leaf-like bracts characteristic of the genus. Flowering dates include June-July. FRUITS are achenes in a deep green globular head. Its color and mace-like shape is easily noticed in aspen poplar woods in August. LEAVES are light green, covered with fine hairs and grow up from the short stem with long petioles. They may be 1½ to 2½ inches (4-7 cm) wide, and are toothed and deeply cleft into three to five lobes. GROWTH HABIT is perennial and the slightly hairy stems grow from a bulb-like taproot. Total plant height varies from 8 to 24 inches (20-60 cm). Common HABITAT includes moist grassy areas, scrubby areas, edges of aspen poplar groves, particularly in parkland-prairie, but the plant is distributed throughout the area in suitable locations.

Canada anemone

CUT-LEAVED ANEMONE
Anemone multifida Poir.

Cut-leaved anemone

flower detail

FLOWERS are usually pink or reddish purple with some variation to yellow or nearly white. Each flower may be ½ to ¾ inches (12-20 mm) across and there are one to seven hairy flowering stalks which arise from the characteristic whorl of bracts below them. Flowers bloom June-July. FRUITS are achenes borne in a cylindrical head, ½ to 1 inch (12-25 mm) long, which is gray green and opens to give a "cottony" appearance due to the soft hairy achenes. LEAVES are silky hairy, 1¼ to 2½ inches (3-7 cm) across, dusty dark green, and divided into three parts. GROWTH HABIT is erect and somewhat less bushy than the Canada anemone, (*A. canadensis* L.), partly due to leaves and partly to the longer flower stalks of the cut-leaved anemone. HABITAT includes the open grasslands of the south central and southwest regions of the area in soils of reasonably good moisture supply.

Cut-leaved anemone

PRAIRIE CROCUS
Anemone patens L. var. *wolfgangiana* (Bess.) Koch.

Prairie crocus

Prairie crocus

seed stage

This is the floral emblem of Manitoba. FLOWERS are pale blue or mauve, occasionally white or light yellow, up to 1½ inches (4 cm) in diameter when open, borne on stems about 4 inches (10 cm) high. The sepals, five to seven, are colored and petals are absent. Flowers appear in early spring. The FRUIT is a large group of feathery achenes on a lengthened flower stalk. LEAVES are gray green, basal, stalked, and much divided. They appear after the flowers fade. GROWTH HABIT is perennial and leaves arise from a thick, woody taproot. Plants persist into September. Common HABITAT includes sandy hillsides and high meadows of the open prairie, and sandy ridges of the parkland.

SMALL-FLOWERED COLUMBINE
Aquilegia brevistyla Hook.

Small-flowered columbine

seed pods

FLOWERS are blue and light cream nearer the centers, ⅝ to 1 inch (1.5-2.5 cm) long and ½ inch (12 mm) or more across, with a single flower on each long, drooping stalk. The five sepals give the blue color and the tube shaped petals supply the white color in the flower. The petals each end in a spur but the blade of the petal is longer than the spur. Flowers appear June-July. FRUIT is a pod, ¼ inch (6 mm) across and about ¾ inch (2 cm) long. The pods are in a tight group of five. LEAVES are dark green and slightly toothed, divided into three pointed leaflets. They are basal but grow up for 8 inches (20 cm) or more with long petioles. GROWTH HABIT is perennial; the slightly hairy, rather thin glandular stems grow from branching rootstocks to a height of 12 to 24 inches (30-60 cm). The flower stalks rise above the leaves for 8 inches (20 cm) or more. Common HABITAT includes the sunny spaces of the moist forest edges and road edges across the north and eastern sections of the area.

Small-flowered columbine

WILD COLUMBINE
Aquilegia canadensis L.

Wild columbine

flower detail

FLOWERS appear deep red due to the five sepals. The tube-like petals are yellow, tinged with red. They are 1 to 1½ inches (2.5-4 cm) across, nodding and up to 1½ inches (4 cm) long. This length includes the spurs which are straight and shorter than the petals. Flowers appear June-July. FRUIT is made up of five follicles, ¼ inch (6 mm) across and about ¾ inch (2 cm) long, with numerous black seeds. LEAVES are compound, divided into three dark green leaflets, usually with some smoothness or bloom. Leaflets may be an inch (2.5 cm) wide and over an inch (2.5 cm) long, slightly toothed and pointed at the apex. GROWTH HABIT is erect, 1 to 3 feet (30-90 cm) high, with a stout stem that may be hairy or smooth. Plants are usually somewhat branched. HABITAT commonly includes the forest edges and roadsides of the north and east, either in open spaces or partial shade, under less moist conditions than where the blue columbine, (*A. brevistyla* Hook.), is common.

Wild columbine

MARSH-MARIGOLD
Caltha palustris L.

Marsh-marigold

Marsh-marigold

flower detail

FLOWERS are deep yellow orange ¾ to 1½ inches (2-4 cm) across, with several attached at the ends of each main stem. The two outer floral rings are not separated, but the color is uniform in the five to nine sepals. There are no true petals. The stamens are numerous and the pistil has several parts. Flowering dates include May-June. FRUITS are in a dense head of many pods which are filled with small seeds. LEAVES are dark green and thick, 1½ inches (4 cm) across. They are kidney-shaped and their bases are heart-shaped. Margins are round-toothed. GROWTH HABIT is perennial and erect, although the plants are rather squat. Height is 8 to 20 inches (20-50 cm), usually nearer 8 inches (20 cm). HABITAT includes stream edges, patches of shallow open water and roadside ditches. This plant is common throughout the north and east parts of the area, particularly where the vegetation is boreal in nature.

PURPLE CLEMATIS
Clematis verticellaris DC.

Western clematis

FLOWERS are blue, 1 to 2 inches (3-5 cm) long, star-shaped with four blue petal-like sepals and no petals. They are borne singly, and appear in June. Flowers of western clematis, (*C. ligusticifolia* Nutt.), which flowers in late July, are white and arranged in a small cluster. FRUITS are hairy achenes with persistent feathery styles, each about 2 inches (5 cm) long. They are grouped in a head. LEAVES are alternate, medium to light green, divided into three stalked leaflets which are arranged in a pinnate fashion on the main stalk. LEAVES may be 3 to 5 inches (7.5-12 cm) long. GROWTH HABIT is trailing, up to 7 feet (2 m) in length, attached to shrubs and small trees. A leafy vine gives the impression of dense growth. HABITAT includes forest and forest margins throughout the south and southwest. Both the purple and white species are common in this area.

Purple clematis

Purple clematis

LOW LARKSPUR
Delphinium bicolor Nutt.

Low larkspur

FLOWERS have dark blue as the prominent color due to five petal-like sepals. The four petals are blue to creamy white and somewhat hairy. The flowers are spurred, ½ to 1¼ inches (12-30 mm) long, borne in a loose spike, May-June. FRUITS are arranged in a head of a few many-seeded pods. The pods are brown, somewhat hairy, ⅝ to ¾ inch (1.5-2 cm) long. LEAVES are more or less basal, medium green and covered with fine hairs which give them a grayish appearance. They are on long stalks and are much cleft and dissected. GROWTH HABIT is perennial and erect from a thick fibrous root. The flower stalks are long and hairy and give the plant a height of 8 to 20 inches (20-50 cm). HABITAT includes sheltered open places in coulees, lower slopes of hills, particularly in the heavier soils of the southwest. The plant is very poisonous to cattle, but is not known to be poisonous to sheep. Take care! Tall larkspur, (*D. glaucum* S. Wats.), is occasionally observed in the aspen poplar stands of some areas of the southwest and northwest. It is also very poisonous to cattle.

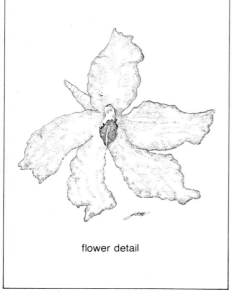

flower detail

Low larkspur

SEASIDE BUTTERCUP
Ranunculus cymbalaria Pursh

Macoun's buttercup

flower detail

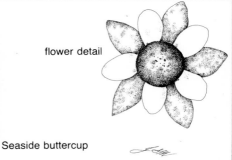

Seaside buttercup

FLOWERS are yellow, few per plant, ¼ to ⅓ inch (6-8 mm) in diameter with petals slightly shorter than the green sepals. They have the conical arrangement of stamens and pistil characteristic of buttercups, and are borne on rather long flower stalks. The other species shown is Macoun's buttercup, (*R. macounii* Britt.), named for John Macoun, an early naturalist who travelled in Saskatchewan. Its flowers are larger, ½ inch (12 mm) and the sepals are reflexed. Approximate flowering date is June. FRUIT is small achenes which are distinctly ribbed longitudinally, formed in an oblong to cylindrical head. LEAVES are medium green, few, small, ½ to 1 inch (12-25 mm) wide, round-toothed and mostly basal. They have rather long petioles and are ovate to heart-shaped. GROWTH HABIT is somewhat creeping with runners which root at the nodes. Plants are rarely over 3 inches (7.5 cm) in height. Stems may be smooth or hairy. HABITAT includes slough margins, creek banks and ravines, with the plant usually found in soggy ground under soil conditions which may be saline. It is widely distributed in the area.

PRAIRIE BUTTERCUP
Ranunculus rhomboideus Goldie

Prairie buttercup

Prairie buttercup

FLOWERS are light yellow with a smooth "painted" look to the five petals which are somewhat narrow and widely spaced. The five shorter sepals are yellow also, often tinged with a lavender shade. They are ½ to ¾ inch (12-20 mm) across and relatively numerous. Flowers appear in early May. FRUITS are achenes in a globular head about 3/16 inch (5 mm) in diameter. LEAVES are dark green, rounded or oval, wavy-margined, over 1 inch (2.5 cm) wide. Basal leaves are spoon-shaped,not divided and have long petioles. The stem leaves are stalkless and deeply cleft into three to five linear lobes. In contrast, on shining-leaved buttercup, (*R. glaberrimus* Hook.), even some of the basal leaves are cleft into lobes; the petals are not as narrow and are closer together. GROWTH HABIT is erect, usually low but may grow to 18 inches (45 cm) in rare cases. Stems are densely hairy. Both species flower early in the spring but the shining-leaved buttercup is lower growing and confined to the southwest. HABITAT includes the lower areas of grasslands, not necessarily at slough margins. It is widely distributed over the grassland and parkland borders of the area.

Shining-leaved buttercup

WHITE WATERCROWFOOT
Ranunculus subrigidus W. B. Drew

White watercrowfoot

FLOWERS are white, with five petals and five sepals, and about ½ inch (12 mm) diameter. They float on the surface of the water or rise only about an inch (2.5 cm) above it, and appear in June. Numerous stamens give the center a yellow color. FRUITS are small achenes arranged in a head. LEAVES are medium green, ½ to 1 inch (12-25 mm) long, finely dissected and all submerged. GROWTH HABIT is perennial and floating, with many long branches which spread it out in a mat at the water surface. The large number of white flowers gives the impression of total coverage in some parts of sloughs. HABITAT includes shallow sloughs, saline or fresh, where there is some slow movement of water. A yellow species, (*R. gmelinii* DC.), is not the source of yellow color in the same sloughs as white watercrowfoot. This deep yellow is due to common bladderwort, (*Utricularia vulgaris* L.).

White watercrowfoot

Yellow watercrowfoot

GOLDEN CORYDALIS
Corydalis aurea Willd.

Golden corydalis

flower detail

Pink corydalis

FLOWERS are deep yellow, about ½ inch (12 mm) long, and sac-like with a spur at the base about ¼ inch (6 mm) long. The spur arises from one of the four petals. There are only two sepals. Another species has pink flowers: *C. sempervirens* (L.) Pers. Flowers bloom in June. FRUIT is a narrow constricted pod-like capsule, ¾ to 1 inch (2-2.5 cm) long, which contains several dark shiny seeds. LEAVES are alternate, pale green, 2½ to 3½ inches (7-10 cm) long, compounded of many fine divisions. GROWTH HABIT is annual or biennial, low or nearly prostrate and much branched. Plants may spread over an area 12 to 18 inches (30-45 cm) across. HABITAT includes forest edges, road cuts, railway grades and other disturbed ground. It is found in the Qu'Appelle Valley and tributaries and up into the edge of the boreal forest as well. Here it is replaced by the pink species, which is taller, less bushy and later in flowering habit.

PINK BEE-PLANT
Cleome serrulata Pursh

Pink bee-plant

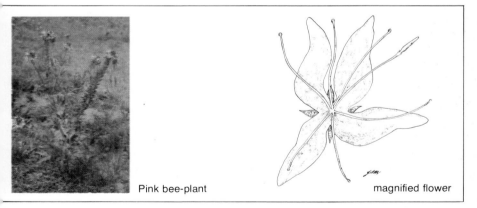

Pink bee-plant   magnified flower

FLOWERS are lavender pink to white, ½ inch (12 mm) long, 1/16 inch (1 mm) diameter, in a nearly globose terminal raceme. The white stamens usually protrude from each flower. Approximate date of flowering is August. FRUIT is a long pod. These pods are evident on the lower parts of the raceme while the upper portion is still in flower. LEAVES are dark green, numerous, alternate, lanceolate, 1 to 3 inches (2.5-7 cm) long. Upper leaves are virtually stalkless. They are not toothed. GROWTH HABIT is annual and erect. Some plants are branched but others have a solitary stem. HABITAT includes waste places, roadsides and semi-cultivated areas of the prairies and the edge of the parkland.

PITCHERPLANT
Sarracenia purpurea L.

Pitcherplant

This is the floral emblem of Newfoundland. FLOWERS are reddish purple due to incurved petals, nodding and borne singly on long stalks. The pistil is greenish yellow and the style is very large. Flowers appear June-July. FRUIT is a capsule, ½ to ¾ inch (12-20 mm) diameter, divided into several sections. LEAVES are bluish green with reddish veins. They are basal and pitcher-shaped, 3 to 12 inches (7.5-30 cm) long with a hood surrounded by downward pointing bristles. The bristles and the pool of water in the leaf tend to trap insects. GROWTH HABIT is basal, perennial, with leaves and the long flower stem arising from the root crown. The flower stalk may be 10 to 18 inches (25-45 cm) high. HABITAT includes black spruce bogs and other spongy areas of coniferous woods in the northeast.

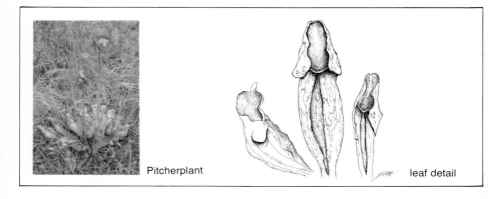

Pitcherplant   leaf detail

ALUMROOT
Heuchera richardsonii R. Br.

Alumroot

FLOWERS are purple to violet, under ⅛ inch (3 mm) diameter, ⅜ inch (10 mm) long, with five petals only slightly longer than the sepals. They are in a dense spike at the end of a long leafless flower stalk and bloom in June. FRUIT is a capsule with two distinct beaks. LEAVES are basal, dark green, leathery, and have long petioles. They are round to heart-shaped and roughly toothed, 1 to 2½ inches (2.5-6 cm) across. GROWTH HABIT is erect and perennial, with basal leaves and several long flower stalks arising from a scaly rootstock. HABITAT includes all reasonably moist areas of the prairie and open parkland. It is named for the explorer, Sir John Richardson.

Alumroot

flower stalk

GRASS-OF-PARNASSUS
Parnassia palustris L.

Grass-of-parnassus

Grass-of-parnassus

flower and leaf

FLOWERS have five wide white petals with distinct green veins. They are large, up to an inch (2.5 cm) across, with sepals much smaller than petals. There are usually several flower stems per plant. Flowers appear July-September. FRUIT is an oval capsule, about ⅜ inch (1 cm) long with many seeds. LEAVES are broad, round, glossy, light green with smooth margins. They are somewhat heart-shaped and basal. A single leaf one-third to one-half way up the flower stalk characterizes this species. GROWTH HABIT is perennial and branching from a tuft of rather fibrous roots. Plant height is due to the flower stalk and varies from 4 to 14 inches (10-35 cm). HABITAT includes wet shady areas at the edge of aspen poplar groves, road ditches and railway grades. It is widely distributed, particularly in the north, central and eastern parts of the area.

WILD BLACK CURRANT
Ribes americanum Mill.

Wild black currant

fruit detail

FLOWERS are greenish white to cream color, with five petals and five stamens. The calyx is tubular. Flowers are numerous, eight to twenty, arranged in many drooping racemes, appearing in June. Flowers of the northern gooseberry, (*R. oxyacanthoides* L.), are also illustrated. FRUIT is a round berry, 3/16 to 3/8 inch (4-10 mm) in diameter, reddish brown as it begins to ripen and black when ripe. It is not particularly palatable raw but makes excellent jelly or jam. LEAVES are alternate, bright green, toothed and divided into three to five lobes. They are heart-shaped at the base and 1 to 3 inches (2.5-8 cm) across. GROWTH HABIT: An erect shrub, branched from the base, 3 to 4 feet (90-120 cm) high. Stems are smooth and there may be fifteen to twenty-five of them in a plant. Several other black currants are also native to the area. Common HABITAT includes edges of aspen poplar groves and patches of scrub in the parkland, and the wooded ravines of the prairies.

Northern gooseberry

SWAMP RED CURRANT
Ribes triste Pall.

fruit detail

Swamp red currant

FLOWERS are purplish pink, several shades deeper in color than those of the wild black currant, (*R. americanum* Mill.). Sepals, (five), are longer than the petals. Flowers are borne on short stalks in a raceme, 2 to 4 inches (5-10 cm) long, and bloom in June. FRUIT is a smooth, round, bright red berry, 3/16 inch (4 mm) diameter. It has a tart pleasant taste and may be preserved as fruit or jelly. LEAVES are alternate, medium green and paler beneath due to fine hairs. They are three to five lobed and coarsely toothed, 2 to 4 inches (5-10 cm) across, on petioles about an inch (2.5 cm) long. GROWTH HABIT: A small bush up to 3 feet (90 cm) tall with many short, unarmed stems arising from the root crown. HABITAT includes low marshy ground near the edges of aspen poplar groves, in the northern edge of the parkland and in the boreal forest.

Swamp red currant

SASKATOON
Amelanchier alnifolia Nutt.

Saskatoon

Saskatoon

fruit stages

FLOWERS are white, ⅜ to ½ inch (9-12 mm) diameter with five rounded petals and five sepals. They are borne in multiple clusters at the ends of branches and appear in June. FRUIT is a berry-like pome, variable in size, over ⅜ inch (1 cm) diameter, reddish purple, ripening to a dark purple. It is sweet and useful as food for people and for much of the native wildlife. It is also known as June-berry and service-berry. LEAVES are simple, stalked, round to oval, ½ to 2 inches (12-48 mm) long and finely toothed, particularly towards the apex. GROWTH HABIT is very variable from a small shrub under a foot (30 cm) tall to small trees of 15 feet (4.5 m). It is usually much branched, particularly at the top. HABITAT includes the margins and interiors of aspen poplar bluffs or scrubby areas of the parkland and forest edges, as well as the moist ravines of the prairies.

HAWTHORN
Crataegus spp. L.

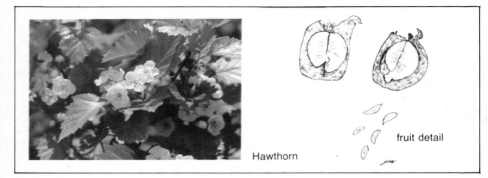

Hawthorn

fruit detail

FLOWERS are white in all four species native to Saskatchewan. There are five sepals, five petals and numerous stamens. Clusters contain six to fifteen flowers, each about ½ inch (12 mm) across. Flowering occurs from May-June. FRUIT is a round, red, berry-like pome, with many seeds and little flesh. Skin color is purplish black in one species, *C. douglasii* Lindl., found in the Cypress Hills. LEAVES are dark green, alternate, doubly toothed and sometimes lobed. Leaves of the Columbian hawthorn, (*C. columbiana* Howell), are distinctly lobed and more obovate than those of the round-leaved hawthorn, (*C. chrysocarpa* Ashe). GROWTH HABIT: Columbian hawthorn is a tall shrub; the round-leaved species is more bushy. The stems are armed with stout thorns of about 1¼ to 2½ inches (3-7 cm). The main trunk may be up to 2 inches (5 cm) diameter, although most are about ¾ inch (2 cm). Height is variable up to 12 feet (4 m). HABITAT includes open woodland, coulees, margins of aspen poplar groves, or as a component of "scrubby" patches throughout the entire area. It is most common where moisture conditions are relatively good.

Hawthorn

SMOOTH WILD STRAWBERRY
Fragaria glauca (S. Wats.) Rydb.

Smooth wild strawberry

Smooth wild strawberry

Smooth wild strawberry

FLOWERS are white, ¾ inch (2 cm) diameter with a yellow center due to numerous stamens. There are several in a loose cluster. Stems lengthen as the fruit matures and raise it off the ground. Flowering is from May-July. FRUIT is an enlarged receptacle in which are embedded numerous dry achenes. A second species, American wild strawberry, (*F. vesca* L. var. *americana* Porter), is known in the northeast and is characterized by a lighter red, more conical fruit, with achenes nearer the surface. LEAVES are dark green, alternate, broadly ovate and coarsely toothed, three-lobed and up to 3 inches (7.5 cm) wide. They may be slightly hairy on the underside. GROWTH HABIT is basal from a rootstock. There are running stems which will send out roots. Leaf petioles and stems of fruit clusters may be 2 to 5 inches (5-12.5 cm) high depending on the habitat. HABITAT includes open shade to full sun in scrubby patches, aspen poplar groves, roadside ditches, wooded ravines, wherever moisture conditions are relatively favorable.

PURPLE AVENS
Geum rivale L.

flower detail

Purple avens

FLOWERS are conspicuously purple due to sepals, with the five petals more yellow with purple streaks. Stamens are numerous. Flowers appear in July. FRUITS are achenes in a bur-like head. LEAVES are basal and along the stem. The basal leaves are petioled, up to 15 inches (37 cm) long. The smaller stem leaves are divided into threes, the terminal segment of which is three-lobed. They are coarsely toothed, dark green and somewhat hairy. GROWTH HABIT is erect and perennial, a hairy stem with few branches, rising from a thick rootstock, not as large or conspicuous as that of three-flowered avens, (*G. triflorum* Pursh). Plants may be 1 to 3 feet (30-90 cm) in height. HABITAT is wet swampy ground in the north and east and in the Cypress Hills.

Purple avens

THREE-FLOWERED AVENS
Geum triflorum Pursh

Three-flowered avens

FLOWERS are reddish purple, due to sepals, ½ to ¾ inch (12-20 mm) across, nodding, and appear in threes at the end of a long flower stem. There are five smaller yellowish petals. Several flowering stems may grow from one rootstock. Flowers appear May-June. FRUITS are achenes with feathery styles about 1 inch (2.5 cm) long, grouped in a dense head. The styles persist until midsummer and are responsible for the name of "old man's whiskers." LEAVES are mostly basal, dark green, compound pinnate and finely toothed. Leaves may have ten to twenty leaflets. There is usually a small tuft of leaves halfway up the flower stem. GROWTH HABIT is basal with flower stems and leaves growing from a coarse black horizontal rootstock. Leaves may be 6 to 8 inches (15-20 cm) long and flower stems may attain a height of 6 to 18 inches (15-45 cm). Flowers appear to be barely open but they are mature at this stage. HABITAT includes open prairie, usually near trees and scrub, where plants grow in patches of ten to several hundred.

Three-flowered avens

Three-flowered avens

SILVERWEED
Potentilla anserina L.

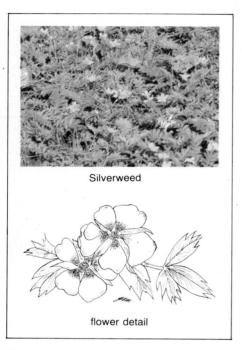

Silverweed

flower detail

FLOWERS are bright yellow, up to 1 inch (2.5 cm) in diameter, with five petals and five sepals. They are borne singly on a long stalk, and appear May-September. The FRUITS are small achenes in a head. LEAVES are basal, compound (seven to twenty-five leaflets), gray green on the upper surface and whitish and woolly underneath; hence the common name for this cinquefoil species. GROWTH HABIT is prostrate or nearly so, tufted, spreading by reddish runners. A similar species, early cinquefoil, (*P. concinna* Richards.), lacks runners and its leaves are a brighter green. HABITAT includes slough margins and other wet places, barnyards, roadside ditches, etc. It is widely distributed throughout the area.

Early cinquefoil

WHITE CINQUEFOIL
Potentilla arguta Pursh

White cinquefoil

FLOWERS are creamy white with a yellow center due to the numerous stamens. The five sepals are green and ovate and they elongate as the fruit matures. Several flowers, ½ to ¾ inch (12-20 mm) across, are borne in a rather crowded cyme, appearing June-July. FRUIT is a light brown achene with visible ridges in its surface. LEAVES are bright green, pinnately compound, with lower leaflets smaller than the upper ones. There are seven to eleven toothed, hairy leaflets on the basal leaves and three to five on the upper ones. Leaflets average about ½ inch (12 mm) in length, but some are over an inch (2.5 cm). GROWTH HABIT is perennial, erect and slightly branching, 12 to 30 inches (30-75 cm) high, but the whole plant gives the appearance of a single stem. HABITAT includes moist low-lying places in the prairie grasslands, slough margins and aspen poplar groves of the area, particularly in the south and central portions.

White cinquefoil

flower detail

SHRUBBY CINQUEFOIL
Potentilla fruticosa L.

Shrubby cinquefoil

Shrubby cinquefoil

Prairie cinquefoil

FLOWERS are deep yellow, ¾ to 1 inch (2-2.5 cm) across with five petals and five sepals. They are borne in small dense clusters, mainly at the ends of branches, from June-August. FRUITS are achenes in a head which is densely hairy. LEAVES are alternate, gray green, with pinnate leaflets compounded in a spreading arrangement of about five leaflets closely attached to the axis. GROWTH HABIT: A bushy shrub with most branches arising from branching rootstocks and growing to 12 to 48 inches (30-120 cm) high. HABITAT includes the low moist areas of sandy soil and lower slopes of sandy areas of the south and southwest. Another yellow species, prairie cinquefoil, (*P. pensylvanica* L.), is illustrated on this page because it is often found associated with shrubby cinquefoil.

PIN CHERRY
Prunus pensylvanica Lf.

Pin cherry

Pin cherry

Pin cherry

FLOWERS are white, ¼ inch (6 mm) diameter, with five petals and five sepals; stamens extend beyond petals. Flowers are short-lived and sepals drop before petals. Flowers are arranged in a round cluster and appear at the time the leaves come out, May-June. The FRUIT is a small, ¼ inch (6 mm) round drupe with a large stone. It is sour but the flavor of jelly made from it is a rare treat. LEAVES are bright green, shiny, alternate, lance-shaped and finely toothed, usually 2 to 6 inches (5-15 cm) long.

GROWTH HABIT: A small tree with a round pattern of many top branches, very variable in height but commonly about 10 feet (3 m) tall. HABITAT includes the open areas of woodlands in the parkland region, as well as wooded coulees and road edges or deeper ravines. It is also found in moist upland depressions in the southwest.

RED CHOKE CHERRY
Prunus virginiana L.

Black choke cherry

Red choke cherry

Red choke cherry

FLOWERS are white, ⅜ to ½ inch (1-1.5 cm) in diameter, with five petals and five sepals. The sepals soon fall. Flowers are borne on short stems in dense cylindrical clusters, May-June. FRUIT is a fleshy drupe with a fairly large stone. It is dark red but bluish black in the commoner variety, *(var. melanocarpa* [A. Nels.] Sarg.). The fruits of both show the same red color in ripening stages. They are edible, particularly as jelly. LEAVES are alternate, dark green above, lighter underneath, egg-shaped or broadly oval, smooth on both sides and sharply toothed. They are 1 to 3 inches (2.5-7.5 cm) long and relatively numerous. GROWTH HABIT is perennial in a range from a low bush to a small tree of 1½ inch (4 cm) diameter and a height of 6 to 12 feet (2-4 m). The black-fruited variety tends to grow taller than the red-fruited one. Common HABITAT includes the edges of wooded areas in the parkland, scrubby patches and deep ravines of the area up to the edge of the boreal forest.

PRICKLY ROSE
Rosa acicularis Lindl.

Prickly rose   ripe fruit

This is the floral emblem of Alberta. FLOWERS are a deep rose red, usually borne singly, 2-3 inches (5-7.5 cm) across, often a deeper color and with less tendency to fade than other native species. However, the color is highly variable. Flowers appear June-July. FRUIT is bright red when ripe, globular in the commonest Saskatchewan variety, (*bourgeauiana*), egg-shaped in another, with the neck constricted in both.

LEAVES are dark green, alternate, compound pinnate, with five to seven leaflets. GROWTH HABIT: A bush with several main stems and many branches, up to 4 feet (120 cm) in height. Stems are thickly covered with weak bristles. Common HABITAT includes the margins of aspen groves, scrubby patches in prairie, coulees and roadsides throughout western Canada.

Prickly rose

PRAIRIE ROSE
Rosa arkansana Porter

Prairie rose

FLOWERS are pink but may fade to white, or petals may be streaked with darker pink. They are usually 1¼ to 2½ inches (3-7 cm) diameter and are in a cluster of two to three blooms. The flowers are much flatter when open than those of the Wood's rose, (*R. woodsii* Lindl.), which are distinctly saucer-shaped and usually a deeper pink. Flowers appear June-August. FRUIT is a hip, almost globular and about ½ inch (12 mm) diameter. It is bright red when ripe and contains many seeds. LEAVES are medium green, pinnately compound, with nine to eleven leaflets which are smooth and shiny. GROWTH HABIT: A low branching shrub, 6 to 18 inches (15-45 cm) high, which dies off to the ground each fall. HABITAT includes open prairie, uncultivated fields and road edges. The plant is most common in the grasslands but persists into the parkland.

Prairie rose

Wood's rose

WILD RED RASPBERRY
Rubus idaeus L. var. *strigosus* (Michx.) Maxim.

Wild red raspberry

Wild red raspberry

Cloudberry

FLOWERS are white, ⅝ inch (15 mm) across, with five petals, five sepals and numerous stamens. They are mainly borne at the ends of stems in several loose clusters. The cloudberry or baked-apple berry, *R. chamaemorus* L.), has similar flowers and a yellowish red fruit like a raspberry. It is shorter and its few leaves arise from the rootstock. Flowers bloom in July. FRUIT is a berry of many fleshy druplets, ½ to ¾ inch (12-20 mm) in diameter. It is bright red when ripe. LEAVES are alternate, compound pinnate with five ovate leaflets, the terminal one of which is usually three-lobed. Leaflets may be up to 4 inches (10 cm) long, toothed, and pointed at the apex. GROWTH HABIT is perennial or biennial, a shrub 3 to 4 feet (90-120 cm) high. Stems are heavily bristled and some thicker stems live beyond the second year. HABITAT includes roadside ditches, cut over and burned land, coulees, etc., throughout the area but the plant is more common in the parkland and the edges of the boreal forest. Although not considered to have an economic value, it has been a valuable addition (raw and preserved) to the diets of many people ever since man came to the plains of North America.

DEWBERRY
Rubus pubescens Raf.

Dewberry

flower detail

Stemless raspberry

FLOWERS are white or pale pink, 3/16 to ⅝ inch (4-15 mm) across, in groups of two or three. Sepals, (five), are reflexed and are clearly visible in this state at the base of the fruit. Flowers are open, as shown in the sketch, for only a short period, and the semi-closed stage is the one most commonly observed. Flowers may appear June-July. FRUIT is a dark red edible berry, ⅜ to ⅝ inch (10-15 mm) across, not easily freed from the receptacle like that of the wild red raspberry, (*R. idaeus* L. var. *strigosus* [Michx.] Maxim.). LEAVES are alternate, light green, smooth and doubly toothed. They are compound, 3 to 4 inches (7-10 cm) across, with three to five ovate leaflets. GROWTH HABIT is trailing or climbing, with stems up to 3 feet (90 cm) but usually under 1 foot (30 cm). Flowers arise from nodes of runners or from the crown of the plant. In general appearance it is much like the stemless or Arctic raspberry, (*R. acaulis* Michx.), which has a purple pink flower and grows on the parkland-forest border and north from there. HABITAT includes deep aspen poplar woods and thickets of heavy scrub in the parkland. It also appears in the Cypress Hills.

NARROW-LEAVED MEADOWSWEET
Spiraea alba Du Roi

Shiny-leaved meadowsweet

magnified flower —
Narrow-leaved meadowsweet

FLOWERS are white, ⅛ inch (3 mm) diameter, with five petals and five sepals. The dense terminal raceme of many flowers gives the impression of a white brush. Flowers bloom in July. FRUIT is a short, ¼ inch (6 mm), papery pod which opens along one side and usually contains four seeds. LEAVES are dark green, alternate, narrowly lanceolate, coarsely toothed to the apex, pointed at both ends, 1 to 1½ inches (2.5-4 cm) long, paler on the underside. GROWTH HABIT is perennial, a brown stemmed shrub with a few slender branches, arising from a more or less running rootstock. Average height 8 to 30 inches (20-75 cm). Common HABITAT includes the moister areas of the prairie region, roadsides and low scrubby places, particularly in the south and central parts of the area. Another species, shiny-leaved meadowsweet, (*S. lucida* Dougl.), has a flat-topped inflorescence and may be observed in the Cypress Hills.

Narrow-leaved meadowsweet

TWO-GROOVED MILK-VETCH
Astragalus bisulcatus (Hook.) A. Gray

Two-grooved milk-vetch

Two-grooved milk-vetch

seed pods

FLOWERS are deep purple to reddish purple, ½ inch (12 mm) long, 1/16 inch (2 mm) diameter. They are tubular and lipped, with five petals and five shorter sepals. The long dense clusters of twenty to thirty blooms have a characteristic "heavy" odor, and appear in June. The FRUIT is a narrowly oblong pod with two deep grooves. LEAVES are opposite, gray green, compound pinnate with seventeen to twenty-seven elliptic leaflets, each ⅜ to 1 inch (10-25 mm) long. GROWTH HABIT is perennial in dense clumps of many stems from one taproot. Clumps may be up to 3 feet (90 cm) across. Stems are semi-decumbent and may be up to 24 inches (60 cm) high. HABITAT includes the dry southern prairies and coulees but the plant extends into central and eastern parts of the area as well. This species and other *Astragalus* species may be poisonous to cattle and sheep, probably due to their tendency to concentrate selenium.

GROUND-PLUM
Astragalus crassicarpus Nutt.

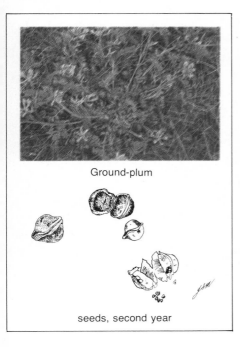

Ground-plum

seeds, second year

FLOWERS are pale violet to white, with the keel distinctly tinged with purple, ½ to ¾ inch (12-20 mm) long. They appear in loose racemes of eight to ten flowers at the ends of stems, May-June. The FRUIT is a pod which is nearly round, ½ inch (12 mm) diameter and reddish when mature, drying to a round, brown, two-valved case containing many black seeds. Pods are usually intact the year following maturity. LEAVES are medium green, numerous, with thirteen to twenty-seven elliptic to oblong leaflets. The leaflets are each ¼ to ⅝ inch (6-15 mm) long, rounded at the apex, smooth on the upper surface but covered with short stiff hairs on the lower surface. GROWTH HABIT is perennial, decumbent in a mat-like arrangement with a mass of fifteen to twenty prostrate stems, each 4 to 18 inches (10-40 cm) long. HABITAT includes the dry plains of the south and southwest extending into similar terrain in the center of the area. It is occasionally called the buffalo-bean.

Ground-plum

NARROW-LEAVED MILK-VETCH
Astragalus pectinatus Dougl.

Narrow-leaved milk-vetch

FLOWERS are cream colored, ½ to 1 inch (12-25 mm) long in short loose clusters of eight to ten flowers, appearing in early June. FRUIT is a broad, oblong, woody pod, ½ to ¾ inch (12-20 mm) long. LEAVES are light green, compound pinnate with nine to nineteen narrow (1 mm) leaflets, each ½ to 2 inches (1-5 cm) long. GROWTH HABIT is semi-erect and much branched with "floppy" red-tinged stems up to 24 inches (60 cm) high. Plants arise from a deep taproot and have a strong tendency to concentrate selenium. They may be poisonous. The purple milk-vetch, (*A. goniatus* Nutt.), is also illustrated here. It is less erect, lower growing and more slender of stem than the narrow-leaved milk-vetch. HABITAT includes light sandy and gravelly soil with the plant often found over marine shales. It is common on the drier prairie and roadsides.

Narrow-leaved milk-vetch

Purple milk-vetch

CUSHION MILK-VETCH
Astragalus triphyllus Pursh

Cushion milk-vetch

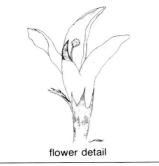

flower detail

FLOWERS are creamy yellow, with a purple area on the keel, ½ to ¾ inch (12-20 mm) long. They are grouped in short clusters buried among the leaves of the plant, and appear May-early June. FRUIT is an oval, silvery-haired pod, partly enclosed by the sepals. LEAVES are gray green, silvery hairy and trifoliate, with leaflets ½ to ¾ inch (12-20 mm) long. Leaves grow up in a clump from the rootstock. GROWTH HABIT: A ball-like mass of leaves and flowers arising from a deep taproot. Total height rarely exceeds 4 inches (10 cm). HABITAT includes the sunny slopes and hillsides of the prairie area, particularly in the south and southwest, but extends to the Qu'Appelle River.

Cushion milk-vetch

WILD LICORICE
Glycyrrhiza lepidota (Nutt.) Pursh

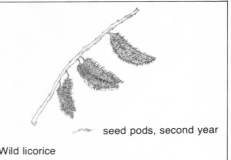

seed pods, second year

Wild licorice

Wild licorice

FLOWERS are yellowish white, somewhat tubular with five petals and five sepals. They are borne on short stalks in dense racemes, 1 to 2 inches (2.5-5 cm) long and appear in July. FRUIT is an oblong brown bur-like pod about ⅜ inch (1 cm) long, densely covered with hooked prickles. The dry stems and pods often persist until the next season. LEAVES are opposite, pale green, compound pinnate with eleven to nineteen glandular-dotted leaflets which are about 1 inch (2.5 cm) long. GROWTH HABIT is perennial, somewhat coarse and starkly erect due to sparse leaves and short branches. The rootstock is thick and has a sweet licorice flavor. HABITAT includes the rough edges of wooded tracts and road and railway grades on wet to moderately dry sandy soils throughout the area. It is somewhat more common in the parkland and forest edge than on the plains.

HEDYSARUM
Hedysarum alpinum L.

Hedysarum

FLOWERS are pinkish to violet, ½ inch (12 mm) long, usually pointing downward in a 3 to 5 inch (7.5-12.5 cm) raceme, appearing June-July. FRUIT is a flat, divided, smooth pod (loment), with slight narrowing between seeds to leave an impression of a sleeve of coins. LEAVES are opposite, medium green, smooth, pinnately compound with eleven to twenty-one oblong leaflets each ½ to 1¼ inches (12-30 mm) long. GROWTH HABIT is perennial, erect with some branching but a slim profile, height 6 to 30 inches (15-75 cm). Some lower seed pods are mature when upper blooms on the same raceme are just beginning to open. HABITAT includes the grassy areas of semi-open prairies, and borders of woodland glades from the south and southwest to the forest edge.

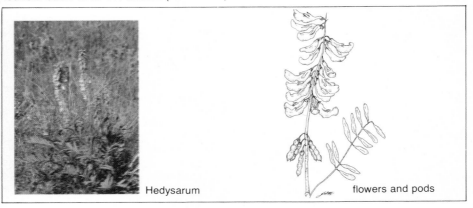

Hedysarum   flowers and pods

WILD PEAVINE
Lathyrus venosus Muhl.

Wild peavine

Wild peavine

FLOWERS are purple with lighter violet areas on some of the petals, ½ to ⅝ inch (12-15 mm) long, typically legume in arrangement. There are twelve to twenty in each dense cluster, appearing June-August. The FRUIT is a dry, thin-walled pod, about 2 inches (5 cm) long, containing four to six seeds. They should be considered poisonous, although the action of poisons of seeds of *Lathyrus* species is not clear. LEAVES are alternate, bright green in a pinnately compound arrangement of eight to twelve oblong ovate, blunt tipped leaflets. Leaves have stipules and terminal tendrils. GROWTH HABIT is perennial and climbing to a length of 1 to 3 feet (30-90 cm). Stems are slightly branched and sometimes rather hairy. HABITAT includes margins of aspen poplar groves and relatively open areas inside such groves, particularly in the north and east. The cream-colored vetchling, (*L. ochroleucus* Hook.), overlaps its range but is more common in the central and western portions.

Cream-colored vetchling

SILVERY LUPINE
Lupinus argenteus Pursh

Silvery lupine   magnified flower

FLOWERS are light blue to violet, ⅜ inch (10 mm) long, ¼ inch (7 mm) across, with five petals and five sepals in the characteristic legume blossom arrangement. The keel is sickle-shaped. They are borne in loose terminal racemes of 2 to 3 inches (5-7.5 cm) in length, from June-July. The FRUIT is an upright silky-hairy pod about an inch (2.5 cm) long. It usually contains four to six seeds. LEAVES are alternate, dark green above, silvery-hairy beneath. The six to nine palmately arranged leaflets may be 1 to 2 inches (2.5-5 cm) long; leaf petioles are long. GROWTH HABIT is perennial and erect, 12 to 24 inches (30-60 cm) high with several hairy branches growing from a scaly branching rootstock. HABITAT includes the Cypress Hills and similar high plains locations in the south and southwest.

Silvery lupine

WHITE SWEET-CLOVER
Melilotus alba Desr.

FLOWERS are white, about 3/16 inch (4 mm) long, densely crowded on an elongated spike-like raceme, 2 to 4 inches (5-10 cm) long. In the yellow species, (*M. officinalis* [L.] Lam.), the standard petal is shorter. Flowers bloom June-August. FRUIT is a rough thick papery pod with one and occasionally two yellow brown seeds. LEAVES are bright green, finely toothed, palmately compound of three leaflets, each ½ to 1 inch (12-25 mm) long. GROWTH HABIT is erect, biennial, and up to 7 feet (2 m) tall on woody, slightly hollow stems. The yellow species is much shorter. Their deep taproots have many branches. HABITAT: This is an introduced plant of some economic importance as cattle feed and as a source of nectar for honey. Its escape to roadside ditches and some fields makes it a pioneer plant of a sort and its appearance and perfume make it a pleasant addition in many places.

White sweet-clover

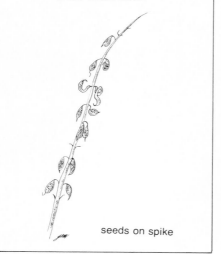

seeds on spike

Yellow sweet-clover

EARLY YELLOW LOCOWEED
Oxytropis macounii (Greene) Rydb.

Early yellow locoweed

Late yellow locoweed

flower detail — Early yellow locoweed

FLOWERS are pale lemon yellow, ⅝ to ¾ inch (1.5-2 cm) long, in a dense spike of six to ten flowers. The spike is more open and flowers larger than in other *Oxytropis* species. Flowers of late yellow locoweed, (*O. gracilis* [A. Nels.] K. Schum), are shorter and creamy yellow in color. Flowers appear in May-June. FRUIT is a hairy short-beaked pod, leathery at maturity, but membranous in late yellow locoweed. LEAVES are all basal, dark gray-green, compound pinnate, silky-hairy but not woolly. The seven to twenty leaflets are oval, ½ to 1 inch (12-25 mm) long. GROWTH HABIT is low, but not densely clumped, and leaves arise from the root crown. Reported to be poisonous to livestock, it is attractive to them because of its early appearance. The late yellow locoweed is taller and flowering stems are longer. HABITAT includes the dry hillsides and open prairies of the south, southwest and central part of the area. The two species combine to provide color in stands of grasses from late May to early September. Early yellow locoweed is often confused with golden-bean, (*Thermopsis rhombifolia* [Nutt.] Richards).

SHOWY LOCOWEED
Oxytropis splendens Dougl.

Showy locoweed

Showy locoweed

detail of spike

FLOWERS are deep blue or purple, ½ inch (12 mm) long in a soft hairy dense spike of eight to twelve flowers. The spike may be 1 to 1½ inches (2.5-4 cm) long. A hairy stem projects it above the leaves. Flowers bloom June-July. Fruit is an ovoid, densely hairy, short-beaked pod, about ½ inch (12 mm) long, held in the floral spike by the sepals. LEAVES are gray green, silky-hairy, basal, numerous, pinnately compound, in a whorled arrangement 3 to 4 inches (7-10 cm) high. GROWTH HABIT is erect and perennial, in a dense clump arising from a thick rootstock, often to a height of 8 to 10 inches (20-25 cm). Several species of locoweed concentrate selenium and are known to be poisonous. HABITAT includes the grasslands of moister areas of the prairies and parkland. The variety *richardsonii* (after Sir John Richardson) has softer, more numerous hairs on leaves and is more common in the extreme southwest. Another similar species, Bessey's locoweed, (*O. besseyi* [Rydb.] Blank.), occasionally appears in the south but it is very rare and worthy of careful identification and preservation.

PURPLE PRAIRIE-CLOVER
Petalostemon purpureum (Vent.) Rydb.

Purple prairie-clover   Purple prairie-clover

White prairie-clover

FLOWERS are numerous, dark to rose purple, small (1 mm), typically legume, in a densely packed terminal head or spike which may be ½ to 1 inch (12-25 mm) long and ¼ inch (6mm) diameter. The flowers are most often observed at the base of the spike with a bare area above, and bloom July-September. FRUIT is a short pod, and there is one of these pods in each depression in the spike. LEAVES are alternate, medium green, and compound pinnate. They are made up of seven to ten narrow, linear leaflets, ¼ to 1 inch (6-25 mm) long and occasionally slightly hairy. GROWTH HABIT is perennial, much branched, usually semi-prostrate, with stems 6 to 24 inches (15-60 cm) long. Two white flowered species, (*P. candidum* [Willd.] Michx. and *P. oligophyllum* [Torr.] Rydb.), are less common but widely distributed in the area. HABITAT is varied but the purple species is commonest on hillsides and uncultivated areas or road edges in the open prairie of the whole southern and central part of the area.

SILVERLEAF PSORALEA
Psoralea agrophylla Pursh

Silverleaf psoralea

Silverleaf psoralea

magnified flower

FLOWERS are deep blue to purple, under ⅛ inch (2 mm) diameter, with unequal lobes extending out of the silvery calyx about ⅛ inch (2 mm). They are arranged in an interrupted spike of one to three whorls. The lance-leaved species, (*P. lanceolata* Pursh), is characterized by pale bluish white flowers in a short dense spike. Both bloom in July. FRUIT is an ovoid silky pod with black seeds. LEAVES are alternate, silvery gray, palmately compound, smooth and hairy on both sides. They are on short petioles about 1¼ inch (3 cm) long and have three to five oblong-ovate leaflets. GROWTH HABIT is perennial and widely branched, often 10 inches (25 cm) high but may be as tall as 40 inches (1 m). Branching is much more open than in Indian breadroot, (*P. esculenta* Pursh), and growth habit is more upright than the lance-leaved species. HABITAT includes the dry uplands of the prairies in the entire southern part of the area, to the edge of the aspen parkland. The lance-leaved species is more common in the southwest.

INDIAN BREADROOT
Psoralea esculenta Pursh

Indian breadroot   mature spike of seeds

FLOWERS are light bluish purple, with five petals and five sepals in typical legume arrangement. They are ½ inch (12 mm) long, usually projecting only 1/16 inch (1 mm) from green, hairy, coarse sepals. The inflorescence is a dense spike 1 to 2 inches (2-5 cm) long. Flowering occurs June-July. FRUIT is a papery long-beaked pod, held among the sepals until maturity when the plants often break off and blow about.

LEAVES are alternate, bright green, compound palmate with five leaflets. They are coarse and hairy, particularly on the underside, with thick hairy petioles. GROWTH HABIT is perennial, bunched in appearance due to branching and compression of leaves to stems. Plants are usually 6 to 12 inches (15-30 cm) high. HABITAT includes high, dry prairie grassland over the south, central and southwest of the area.

Indian breadroot

GOLDEN-BEAN
Thermopsis rhombifolia (Nutt.) Richards.

Golden-bean

flowers and pods

FLOWERS are bright golden yellow, about ½ inch (12 mm) long, with several flowers arranged in a dense terminal spike. This plant is reported to be poisonous, particularly to children, in both the flower and seed stage. Flowering dates range from May-early June. FRUIT is a grayish brown hairy curved pod, about 2 inches (5 cm) long with four to six seeds. LEAVES are alternate, composed of three dark-green ovate leaflets, ¾ to 1¼ inches (2-3 cm) long, with long stalks and large ovate stipules. GROWTH HABIT is perennial and branching, 6 to 20 inches (15-50 cm) high, usually in large patches, growing from running rootstocks. HABITAT includes the moister areas of the prairies, grassy roadside ditches, etc., where the water table is high. It is widely distributed over the southern half of the area.

Golden-bean

RED CLOVER
Trifolium pratense L.

| Red clover | Alsike clover |

FLOWERS are red, (white and pink respectively in the two other species, *T. repens* L. or white Dutch and *T. hybridium* L. or alsike). They are in the typical legume form, each about ¼ to ½ inch (6-12 mm) long in a dense rounded head of fifteen to twenty flowers, appearing in July. FRUIT is a dry pod containing one to six seeds, usually held among the sepals in each section of the rounded head. LEAVES are smooth, dark green, up to ¾ inch (20 mm) long, ¼ inch (6 mm) wide, made up of three oval to elliptic leaflets which are pointed and slightly toothed. GROWTH HABIT is perennial and creeping, usually rather bunched, but some stems may be more than a foot (30 cm) long. HABITAT includes lawns, gardens and field edges where moisture conditions are better than average. The three species illustrated are widely distributed and red clover, (*T. pratense* L.), is more common in Alberta. Like the yellow and white sweet-clovers, they have also escaped to the point of being considered common wildflowers.

White Dutch clover

STICKY GERANIUM
Geranium viscosissimum Fisch. and Mey.

FLOWERS are deep lavender pink, 1¼ to 1½ inches (3-4 cm) across, with five petals and five sepals; the latter are hairy and tipped with awns. There are several blooms in a flat-topped cluster on the glandular, hairy flower stalk. This is the "windflower" of the Cypress Hills that turns meadows deep pink in June of some years. Approximate date of flowering is June-July. FRUITS arise from a stigma that is divided into five carpels, and the long-beaked capsule retains these five divisions, as shown by the sketch of the fruit of Bicknell's geranium, (*G. bicknellii* Britt.). The genus name *Geranium* is derived from the Greek word for crane because the fruit resembles the bill of this bird. LEAVES are opposite medium green, hairy and glandular, 1½ to 4 inches (4-10 cm) wide and three to five times divided into sharply toothed segments. GROWTH HABIT is erect and perennial, with some branching. A height of 12 to 24 inches (30-60 cm) is common HABITAT includes the open areas of wooded uplands, particularly on the south slopes of the Cypress Hills. Bicknell's and the white species, (*G. richardsonii* Fisch and Trautv.), are more common and Bicknell's is relatively common at the north and eastern edges of the boreal forest.

Sticky geranium

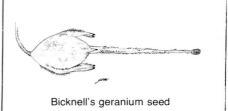

Bicknell's geranium seed

Sticky geranium

WILD BLUE FLAX
Linum lewisii Pursh

Wild blue flax

Wild blue flax   seed capsule

FLOWERS are pale blue, ¾ to 1½ inches (15-35 mm) diameter. The five petals may have radiate lines of lighter blue. Several flowers are borne in a loose terminal cluster, and appear June-July. FRUIT is a round capsule, ⅛ inch (3 mm) diameter, which matures rapidly. LEAVES are linear, ⅜ to ¾ inch (7-15 mm) long, gray green and numerous. GROWTH HABIT is erect and perennial, 10 to 24 inches (25-60 cm) tall with several stems arising from each rootstock. HABITAT includes dry open places, roadsides and railway grades throughout the area; the plant is more common in the south and central part. This plant is named for the American explorer, Capt. Meriwether Lewis of the famed Lewis and Clark expedition.

FRINGED MILKWORT
Polygala paucifolia Willd.

Fringed milkwort

White milkwort

FLOWERS are irregular, rose purple to pink due to two of the five sepals which are petal-like, and three petals each ⅜ to ¾ inch (1-2 cm) long. The keel of the corolla has a fringed crest, at least partly responsible for one of this plant's common names, "gaywings." Three or four flowers are borne in a loose raceme at the end of each stem. Another species, white milkwort, (*P. alba* Nutt.), is occasionally found in more southern parts of the area. Flowering occurs in June. FRUIT is a small two-valved capsule with only two seeds. LEAVES are alternate, entire, upper ones ovate, ⅜ to 1¼ inches (1-3 cm) long, prominently veined on the underside. Lower leaves are small and scale-like. GROWTH HABIT is essentially erect, growing from creeping rhizomes, but stems are weak. Stems are branched and the whole plant is no more than 4 to 7 inches (10-15 cm) high. HABITAT includes sunny open spaces in spruce groves of the boreal forest area. It is fairly common in moist sandy woodlands of the north and east.

Fringed milkwort

POISON-IVY
Rhus radicans L.

Poison-ivy

FLOWERS are yellowish green, small, 1/16 inch (2 mm) long, with five sepals which are joined and slightly shorter than the petals. The five petals are veined with green and there are five stamens. Blooms are grouped in dense panicles in the leaf axils, and appear in early July. FRUITS are round, ¼ inch (6 mm) diameter, a cluster of greenish berries slowly ripening to dull white. LEAVES are alternate, bright green, smooth, up to 4 inches (10 cm) wide, compound, made up of three drooping, strongly-veined leaflets. Remember the saying, "leaves three — let it be." Leaflets are usually notched in an irregular fashion. They turn a brilliant red in the autumn. GROWTH HABIT: A low erect shrub which grows from a creeping rootstock to a height of 4 to 12 inches (10-30 cm). HABITAT includes deep wooded coulees and shady wooded places throughout Western Canada; the plant is very common along the Qu'Appelle River and its tributaries. It is noted for production of a powerful skin poison and irritant. All parts of the plant may exude enough of this poison to affect susceptible persons.

Poison-ivy

magnified flower group

SKUNKBUSH
Rhus trilobata Nutt.

Skunkbush

Skunkbush   ripe fruit

FLOWERS are yellowish green, under ⅛ inch (2 mm) in diameter, in close terminal clusters. The five petals are united. Flowers appear before leaves and persist until the bushes leaf out. Approximate date of the flowering is mid-May. The FRUIT is a globular to coin-shaped dark red berry. LEAVES are dark gray green, alternate and roughly divided into three parts. Each leaflet is ½ to 1¼ inches (12-30 mm) long. GROWTH HABIT: A small bush or several plants in a bushy clump, usually under 3 feet (90 cm) in height and diameter. HABITAT includes south-facing slopes of coulees, particularly those leading into the Qu'Appelle River.

SCARLET MALLOW
Malvastrum coccineum (Pursh) A. Gray

Scarlet mallow   flower detail

FLOWERS are orange red with five petals, five sepals and numerous stamens. The short, dense, leafy spikes have four to six flowers. Flowers appear May-July. FRUIT is formed of the carpels and develops in ten or more papery segments, each of which contains a single seed. LEAVES are alternate and gray green due to a covering of soft white hairs. They are divided into three to five divisions which are each lobed or forked. Each division is ½ to ¾ inches (12-20 mm) wide. GROWTH HABIT is perennial, erect or semi-erect from a thick, scaly rootstock. Plants are 6 to 8 inches (15-20 cm) high, forming a mat of stems with several flowers on each. HABITAT includes roadsides, railway grades and other disturbed places throughout the southern half of the area. It is more common in the southwest. On the open prairie, plants are smaller and more separated. The other mallows, (*Malva* spp.), have been introduced, so this is the only native member of the family.

Scarlet mallow

NORTHERN BOG VIOLET
Viola nephrophylla Greene

Early blue violet

flower detail —
Northern bog violet

FLOWERS are bluish purple, up to ¾ inch (2 cm) across, borne on long stems. Petals are somewhat hairy, particularly the spur petal. It is similar to the early blue violet, (*V. adunca* J. E. Smith), which has somewhat smaller flowers. Flowers appear May-July. FRUIT is a dry, three-valved capsule which breaks open with some force to scatter the fifteen to twenty seeds it may contain. LEAVES are all basal, oval to kidney-shaped, round toothed and wavy margined, heart-shaped at the base and bluntly pointed. There are only a few per plant and they are 1½ to 2½ inches (4-7 cm) wide. GROWTH HABIT is erect, perennial, 2 to 4 inches (5-10 cm) tall to the top of the tallest flower stem. This species has no distinct stem but leaves of the early blue violet grow on a stem which is 1½ to 6 inches (4-15 cm) long. Common HABITAT includes moist edges of aspen poplar groves, sloughs and bogs. It is one of the commonest violets of the plains and forest edges in northern and eastern parts of the area, but only the early blue violet is common in moist locations on the prairie.

Northern bog violet

NUTTALL'S YELLOW VIOLET
Viola nuttallii Pursh

Nuttall's yellow violet

Nuttall's yellow violet

Yellow meadow violet

FLOWERS are deep yellow with five sepals, five petals and five stamens. There is a short spur on the lowest petal. There are four to ten blooms per plant and they arise from the axils of the upper leaves. Another species, yellow meadow violet, (*V. vallicola* A. Nels.), is very similar except for differences in leaves. It is sometimes classed as a variety of *V. nuttallii* Pursh. Flowering occurs May-June. FRUIT is a dry, three-valved, many-seeded capsule. LEAVES are alternate, narrowly lanceolate, 1 to 2½ inches (2.5-7 cm) long, tapering to the stem and slightly hairy. The yellow meadow violet has elliptic basal leaves and ovate to broadly lanceolate stem leaves. Differences in leaf hairs make the yellow meadow violet appear a brighter green. GROWTH HABIT is low, 2½ inches (7 cm) and stems are short, with a clump of narrow dark green leaves topped with a bunch of yellow flowers. Plants of the yellow meadow violet are much less extensive and slightly shorter. HABITAT includes reasonably moist areas of the prairie in the south central and southwest. Two other yellow violets are occasionally observed in eastern parts of the area.

CROWFOOT VIOLET
Viola pedatifida G. Don

Crowfoot violet

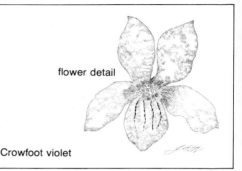

flower detail

FLOWERS are violet blue, large, ¾ inch (2 cm) across, on relatively short stems. The three lower petals are whitest at the base inside and heavily bearded in the cup of the flower. Approximate flowering date is June. FRUIT is a yellowish gray, ¼ inch (6 mm) capsule, which contains several light brown seeds. LEAVES are all basal, stemless, cleft almost to their bases into three lobes which are again divided into three or four lobes; hence, "crowfoot." They may be up to 4 inches (10 cm) wide and are slightly hairy at the margins. GROWTH HABIT is perennial, lacking a stem, with flowers and leaves arising from a short, vertical rootstock to 5 to 7 inches (13-18 cm) height. HABITAT includes grass-covered soil of the open prairie and hillsides where moisture conditions are relatively good. Because of their leaf shape they are rarely noticed in the grass until the flowers come into bloom.

Crowfoot violet

WESTERN CANADA VIOLET
Viola rugulosa Greene

Western Canada violet

seed capsule

FLOWERS are white with pink to purplish veins on petals. Unopened buds are lavender pink with the white inside edges of petals showing. Flowers have five sepals and five petals, one of which has a prominent spur. They may be ½ to 1 inch (12-25 mm) diameter, and appear June-August. FRUIT is a dry, three-valved, many-seeded capsule which is studded with short spines to give it the appearance of a mace. LEAVES are alternate on long stalks, kidney-shaped or heart-shaped, smooth margined and pointed at the apex. They may be over 3 inches (7.5 cm) wide. GROWTH HABIT is erect, 8 to 24 inches (20-60 cm) tall, somewhat decumbent if moisture and light cause the plant to be very tall. This species is probably the longest flowering and most commonly observed violet. It is often called the wood violet. HABITAT includes shady places in aspen poplar groves and scrubby patches, and coulees throughout the entire region where moisture conditions are relatively good.

Western Canada violet

EVENINGSTAR
Mentzelia decapetala (Pursh) Urban and Gilg.

Eveningstar

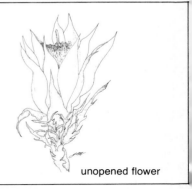

unopened flower

Eveningstar

FLOWERS are creamy white with five sepals and ten petals, five of which are modified sterile stamens. There are numerous fertile stamens and a long thin pistil which persists after the other flower parts have fallen. Flowering occurs July-August. FRUIT is an oblong capsule 1½ inches (4 cm) long, up to ½ inch (12 mm) thick, occasionally covered by leafy bracts as well as sepals. LEAVES are alternate, gray green, oblong-lanceolate, sharply toothed, 2 to 6 inches (5-15 cm) long, covered with soft spine-like white hairs. Lower leaves have short stalks and the upper ones are stalkless. GROWTH HABIT is biennial, a rough branching plant with stout gray green, sticky stems and branches. Height is variable but may commonly range from 6 to 36 inches (15-90 cm). HABITAT includes rough hillsides, clay exposures and badlands in the south and southeast of the area.

PINCUSHION CACTUS
Mamillaria vivipara (Nutt.) Haw.

Pincushion cactus

FLOWERS are violet purple due to sepals and petals, 1½ to 2 inches (4-5 cm) across, with a yellow center due to many stamens. Flowers arise at the convergence of the tubercles of the stem, and appear in July. FRUIT is a pale green fleshy berry which turns brown on ripening. It is edible and sweet but has a very bland flavor. LEAVES are absent; i.e., they are modified into three to eight short (⅛ inch or 3 mm) brownish green spines which cover each of the cone-shaped tubercles of the stem. GROWTH HABIT is perennial, cushion-like or tufted, in a group of branched balls, 1½ to 2 inches (4-5 cm) tall, each composed of several spine-tipped tubercles. HABITAT includes the open prairie, particularly south-facing slopes, of the south and southwest up to and along the Qu'Appelle Valley to the Fishing Lakes.

Pincushion cactus   opened berry

PLAINS PRICKLY-PEAR CACTUS
Opuntia polyacantha Haw.

Plains prickly-pear cactus

opened berry

Plains prickly-pear cactus

FLOWERS are light lemon yellow to pinkish orange, distinctly waxy, 2 to 3 inches (5-7.5 cm) across, with many sepals, petals and stamens. Flowers are numerous and bloom over an extended period, from mid-June to July. FRUIT is a soft, spicy-sweet, edible berry, round to ovate and about 1 inch (2.5 cm) long, filled with large bony discoid seeds (3/16 inch or 5 mm diameter). LEAVES are lacking, having evolved into clusters of five to nine straight spines, ½ to 2 inches (1-5 cm) long, on the surface of the pale green stem. GROWTH HABIT is perennial and prostrate, characterized by large clumps of jointed prickly stems. The brittle prickly-pear, (*O. fragilis* [Nutt.] Haw.), has rounder, more fleshy internodes in its stems. HABITAT includes dry hillsides, on even drier south slopes than those frequented by the pincushion cactus, all over the south, central and southwest of the area.

SILVERBERRY
Elaeagnus commutata Bernh.

Silverberry.   fruit detail

FLOWERS are silvery yellow, ⅛ inch (3 mm) diameter and very fragrant. They are arranged in clusters of three or four, lack petals and have four sepals and four to eight stamens. Flowers bloom in June. FRUIT is a silvery-colored, tough skinned, dry, mealy berry, about ¼ inch (6 mm) in diameter, containing a large stony seed. LEAVES are alternate, silvery gray, scurfy on both sides, oblong to ovate, numerous, 1 to 3 inches (2.5-8 cm) long. GROWTH HABIT is perennial, a low shrub with purplish brown stems, moderately branched, 2 to 12 feet (60 cm - 4 m) high but rarely more than 7 feet (2 m). It is also called wolfwillow. HABITAT includes the moister areas of the plains and the parkland, edges of coulees, etc., in the southern half of the area, particularly where land is overgrazed.

Silverberry

SILVER BUFFALOBERRY
Shepherdia argentea Nutt.

Silver buffaloberry

FLOWERS are brownish yellow, about 1/16 inch (2 mm) diameter, with no petals and four sepals. They are in small clusters at the leaf axils. All flowers on any particular bush will be either male or female, not both. Flowers appear May-June. FRUIT is a round, bright red berry with an insipid taste and is reputed to be useful for jelly after a hard frost. The berry of Canada or russet buffaloberry, (*S. canadensis* [L.] Nutt.), has even less taste. It ripens earlier (July), is less plentiful and is not considered edible. LEAVES are oblong to ovate, 1 to 2 inches (2.5-5 cm) long, densely silvery-scurfy on both sides. They are smooth on the upper surface in russet buffaloberry, sometimes referred to as smooth buffaloberry. GROWTH HABIT: A tall thickly branched perennial shrub with rough spines well distributed along the silvery branches. The total height may be 7 to 15 feet (2-4 m). The russet species is more bushy and stems are not thorny. HABITAT includes wooded coulees and river terraces in the central portion of the area. Both species are often observed in parkland-prairie transition zones, but the russet buffaloberry is more common in the north and east.

Canada buffaloberry

Canada buffaloberry

FIREWEED
Epilobium angustifolium L.

Fireweed

Fireweed

magnified flower

This is the floral emblem of the Yukon. FLOWERS are pink to light purple, rarely white, ½ to 1¼ inches (12-30 mm) diameter, in a long terminal raceme, with a small bract below each flower stalk, appearing July-August. FRUIT is a long narrow capsule, ¾ to 1¼ inches (2-3 cm). Each seed has a tuft of hairs. LEAVES are alternate, lance-shaped, gray green, slightly paler green on the lower side. They are short stalked, have smooth margins and may vary from 2 to 6 inches (5-15 cm) in length. GROWTH HABIT is erect, generally with a single stem dominated by the long terminal raceme. Height is highly variable but usually over 3 feet (90 cm) and under 6 feet (180 cm). HABITAT includes almost any disturbed area, particularly if it has been burned over, from scrubby patches on the prairie to the open parkland and forest.

SCARLET GAURA
Gaura coccinea Pursh

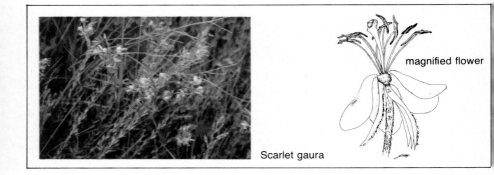

magnified flower

Scarlet gaura

FLOWERS are white on opening but turn scarlet in a few hours. They are usually about ⅜ inch (1 cm) diameter and borne in terminal racemes, appearing June-July. The FRUIT is a nut-like capsule, ¼ inch (6 mm) long, containing few seeds. LEAVES are alternate, somewhat bluish green, oblong to lance-shaped. They lack petioles, are ¾ to 1¼ inch (2-3 cm) long and may be wavy-margined or with shallow teeth. GROWTH HABIT varies from decumbent to erect, usually nearer the former. Plants are 4 to 12 inches (10-30 cm) high. Stems and leaves are covered with fine grayish hairs. Common HABITAT includes the dry prairie, road edges and hillsides of the southern and central parts of the area.

Scarlet gaura

YELLOW EVENING-PRIMROSE
Oenothera biennis L.

Yellow evening-primrose

FLOWERS are bright lemon yellow, 1 to 2 inches (2.5-5 cm) in diameter, with four reflexed sepals and four petals, erect in a long, dense, leafy terminal cluster. All flowers do not bloom at once and they usually open in the evening. Flowers appear July-August. FRUIT is a dry, coarse, slightly hairy, stalkless capsule about 2 inches (5 cm) long, with many small seeds. LEAVES are alternate, lance-shaped to oval, deep green, 1 to 5 inches (2.5-12 cm) long. Those on the lower stem have short stalks but they are stalkless on the upper stem. GROWTH HABIT is bushy and branched from a deep taproot. There are several varieties of this species. Shrubby evening-primrose, (*O. serrulata* Nutt.), is erect or decumbent in growth habit and has yellow flowers, but they resemble the white flowers of the gumbo evening-primrose, (*O. caespitosa* Nutt.), and white evening-primrose, (*O. nuttallii* Sweet), in the fact that they are less tubular and more radiate in shape, and open in the morning. Shrubby evening-primrose tends to occupy the same niches as this species and the white evening-primrose. HABITAT: Both species of yellow evening-primrose appear in field edges and in waste places, particularly in the south central parts of the area.

seed capsule

Yellow evening-primrose

GUMBO EVENING-PRIMROSE
Oenothera caespitosa Nutt.

Gumbo evening-primrose

Gumbo evening-primrose

seed capsule

FLOWERS are white when they open but fade to a delicate pink by the end of the same day. They have four petals, four sepals and eight stamens. Several flowers grow from the root crown, and appear June-August. FRUIT is a stalkless woody capsule arising from the root crown. LEAVES are clustered in a rough rosette on short petioles. They are dark, bright blue green, oblong to lance-shaped, slightly toothed or wavy-margined, 3 to 8 inches (7-20 cm) long. GROWTH HABIT is basal, little more than an inch (2.5 cm) above ground, from a thick woody root. HABITAT includes dry clay slopes and roadcuts throughout the south and central portion of the area, particularly where Cretaceous shales are near the surface.

WHITE EVENING-PRIMROSE
Oenothera nuttallii Sweet

White evening-primrose

White evening-primrose

FLOWERS are white, about 1½ inches (4 cm) across. They usually open in the morning and fade into a light pink by evening. They have a strong, rather unpleasant, heavy scent. The flowers develop in the axils of the upper leaves, and appear in July. FRUIT is a slender, somewhat curved capsule, ¾ to 1¼ inches (2-3 cm) long. LEAVES are alternate, pale green, linear, 1 to 4 inches (3-10 cm) long, with wavy margins and without teeth. GROWTH HABIT is perennial and much branched, 15 to 40 inches (35-100 cm) tall. Stems are white and shiny and have bark that shreds easily. Plants grow from a white, fleshy rootstock. The yellow species shown here is shrubby evening-primrose, (*O. serrulata* Nutt.). Its growth habit is very similar to the white species described. HABITAT includes road edges and margins of fields, particularly in sandy soils in the southern third of the area. It is named for Thomas Nuttall, a naturalist who collected plants in a journey up the Mississippi River in 1811.

Shrubby evening-primrose

WILD SARSAPARILLA
Aralia nudicaulis L.

Wild sarsaparilla

Wild sarsaparilla

Wild sarsaparilla

FLOWERS are greenish white, under ⅛ inch (3 mm) diameter, borne on a flowering stalk 6 to 12 inches (15-30 cm) long, which is usually below the level of the leaves. Early June is the approximate flowering date. FRUIT is a round, purplish black, fleshy berry-like drupe, about ¼ inch (4-6 mm) in diameter, with three distinct compartments. LEAVES are light green on the upper surface and paler below. They are smooth-surfaced with finely-toothed margins. The single leaf stalk grows up for 6 to 12 inches (15-30 cm) and then divides into three parts which divide again into three to five leaflets. They are oval, sharply pointed at the apex, 3 to 5 inches (7-13 cm) long and turn a bronze color in autumn. GROWTH HABIT is perennial from a creeping rootstock. Leaf stem and shorter flower stem extend from a thick root base to 12 to 15 inches (30-40 cm). HABITAT: This plant is a characteristic feature of the understory of parkland groves and wooded ravines of the area in all parts except the extreme south and southwest.

SPOTTED WATER-HEMLOCK
Cicuta maculata L.

Spotted water-hemlock

FLOWERS are white, 1/16 inch (2 mm) diameter, numerous, in a rounded compound umbel which has narrow bractlets at the base of each umbellet, but no bracts at the base of the compound umbel. Flowers appear July-September. FRUIT is oval, about 1/8 inch (4 mm) long, nut-like with five thick ribs on the surface. LEAVES are alternate, compound pinnate, with narrowly lanceolate leaflets which are sharply toothed and 2 to 8 inches (5-20 cm) long. They are conspicuously wider than those of the water-parsnip, (*Sium sauve* Walt.), which are only singly pinnate (see sketch). GROWTH HABIT: A tall branching perennial, usually 1 to 3 feet (30-90 cm) but occasionally to 6 feet (180 cm), which grows from stout, tuberous, bulb-like rootstocks. Stems are smooth. HABITAT includes slough margins, ditches, lake shores, etc., often in association with water-parsnip. Two other species of water-hemlock grow in Saskatchewan, and all parts of the plants of all *Cicuta* species are very poisonous to human beings and livestock. Western water-hemlock, (*C. douglasii* [DC.] Coult. and Rose), replaces spotted water-hemlock in the west.

Spotted water-hemlock

Water-parsnip

COW-PARSNIP
Heracleum lanatum Michx.

Cow-parsnip

Cow-parsnip

flower enlarged

FLOWERS are white, slightly over 1/16 inch (2 mm) in diameter, with petals of varying length. There are hundreds of flowers in the slightly rounded, compound umbel which may be 12 inches (30 cm) across. Flowers bloom June-August. FRUIT is a flattened, oblong-ovate carpel up to ⅜ inch (1 cm) long. The dry umbels and stems are a conspicuous feature of the late fall and winter in the parkland. LEAVES are alternate, hairy, dark green on the upper surface and lighter underneath. They are 4 to 12 inches (10-30 cm) wide, palmately compounded into three toothed and divided leaflets. GROWTH HABIT is perennial, slightly branched, usually over 3 feet (1 m) tall and often up to 8 feet (2.5 m). Stems are hairy, ridged and hollow and may be up to ¾ inch (2 cm) in diameter. HABITAT includes moist open areas in aspen groves and moist meadows and ditches. It is commonest in the aspen parkland and very scarce in the southwest.

LEAFY MUSINEON
Musineon divaricatum (Pursh) Nutt.

Leafy musineon

Hairy-fruited parsley

Musineon flowers and leaf

FLOWERS are powdery yellow with five petals and five sepals, and are supported by linear bractlets. The flowers are borne in a compound umbel, 2 to 2½ inches (5-7 cm) across, and appear in May. FRUIT is ovoid to oblong, 3/16 inch (4 mm) in length, laterally flattened. LEAVES are basal, doubly pinnate, with the main axis more or less winged. Leaflets are oblong, bright green and smooth, in contrast to prairie parsley, (*Lomatium* spp.), which has hairs on stems and leaves. GROWTH HABIT is erect, but low-growing and spreading. Flower heads are not usually more than 4 inches (10 cm) tall and the leaflets are beneath them. Common HABITAT includes the drier areas of the prairies of the south and southwest, usually among grass in well established swards.

HEART-LEAVED ALEXANDERS
Zizia aptera (Gray) Fern.

flowers and leaves

Heart-leaved alexanders

FLOWERS are bright deep yellow, extremely small, under 1 mm in diameter, borne in a very flat, rather open umbel, appearing June-July. FRUIT is a flattened, nut-like, two-seeded capsule and has no ribbing as have fruits of many of the parsley family. LEAVES are bright green, smooth and finely toothed. The upper leaves clasp the stem and are three-lobed and smaller, ¾ to 1¼ inches (2-3 cm) wide. Basal leaves are borne on petioles and are heart-shaped, hence the common name. Another species, golden alexanders, (*Z. aurea* [L.] Koch), is very similar but all leaves are divided like the upper ones of the heart-leaved species. GROWTH HABIT is perennial and erect. Plants are slightly branched and usually 10 to 24 inches (25-60 cm) high. HABITAT includes moist meadows and scrubby margins of aspen poplar groves in the parkland and moister areas of the prairie. Golden alexanders or meadow-parsnip is more eastern in range and its presence in Saskatchewan has not been established with certainty.

Heart-leaved alexanders

BUNCHBERRY
Cornus canadensis L.

Bunchberry

flower detail

FLOWERS appear white due to four large involucral bracts, ½ to ¾ inches (15-20 mm) long, which surround a cluster of minute green flowers. Flowers appear June-July. FRUIT is a small red orange drupe with a two-seeded stone. (The plant is also known as the pigeon berry.) LEAVES are oval, smooth, entire margined, dark green, 1 to 3 inches (2.5-7.5 cm) long and prominently veined. There are four to six leaves in a whorled arrangement at the head of the stem and a pair of smaller leaves halfway down. GROWTH HABIT is perennial, 3 to 6 inches (7.5-15 cm) high, usually forming a dense mat once established in an area by spreading on a slender horizontal rootstock. Common HABITAT includes shady open areas in mixed or coniferous woods or occasionally in moist aspen poplar woods in the central, north and east and in the Cypress Hills.

Bunchberry

RED-OSIER DOGWOOD
Cornus stolonifera Michx.

Red-osier dogwood

Red-osier dogwood

flower, much enlarged

FLOWERS are greenish white, 3/32 inch (1 mm) in diameter, borne in flat-topped cymose clusters of 1 to 2 inches (2.5-5 cm) diameter, with eight to twelve flowers in each. Flowering occurs in June. The FRUIT is a round, whitish, waxy berry, sometimes tinged with blue, about 3/16 inch (4 mm) diameter. It is not edible. LEAVES are opposite, ovate, with a rounded base and pointed apex. They are 1 to 3 inches (2.5-7.5 cm) long, not toothed, deep medium green above and slightly paler beneath due to short hairs on the under-side. GROWTH HABIT: A much branched shrub, 3 to 6 feet (90-180 cm) tall with distinctly reddish bark. Stems are not strong and some bushes appear semi-prostrate. HABITAT includes margins of woodlands and roadsides in the parkland and the coulees of the south and southwest. This is "kinnikinik" to the Crees and the pioneers who settled the parkland, and to those who learned first about plants from either.

ONE-FLOWERED WINTERGREEN
Moneses uniflora (L.) A. Gray

One-flowered wintergreen

flower detail

One-flowered wintergreen

FLOWERS are waxy white, fragrant, nodding and solitary. The five petals are widely spreading so the flower may be ¾ inch (2 cm) across. The pistil is elongated and conspicuous and the ovary is bright green. Flowers appear in July. FRUIT is a dry, brown, erect, many-seeded capsule. LEAVES are dark green, smooth, rounded and finely toothed. They are ½ to 1 inch (12-25 mm) long, borne in pairs or whorls near the base of the stem and remain more or less green in winter. GROWTH HABIT is perennial from a slender rootstock, low but erect, 2 to 6 inches (5-15 cm) tall. HABITAT is the forest floor, usually where conifers predominate, in areas of deep shade and high water table. It is found particularly in the north and east and in the Cypress Hills.

PINK WINTERGREEN
Pyrola asarifolia Michx.

Pink wintergreen

Pink wintergreen

seed capsules

FLOWERS are brownish red, pink when fully opened, about ⅜ inch (1 cm) diameter. They are borne in an open raceme of ten to fifteen flowers which are nodding and characterized by a long protruding style. Flowers appear June-July. FRUIT is a round, dry, many-seeded capsule. LEAVES are basal on short petioles, 1 to 1½ inches (2.5-4 cm) wide, dark green and shiny. They are rounded and stay green into severe autumn frosts. GROWTH HABIT is erect but only the flower-bearing stem rises appreciably above the forest floor. Stalks of the flowers may reach 15 inches (40 cm) but 6 to 8 inches (15-20 cm) is more common. HABITAT includes the forest floor of aspen poplar and mixed woods, where good moisture conditions prevail. It is widely distributed throughout the parklands.

GREENISH-FLOWERED WINTERGREEN
Pyrola chlorantha Sw.

Greenish-flowered wintergreen

White wintergreen (shinleaf)

One-sided wintergreen

FLOWERS are greenish white, (white in shinleaf wintergreen, *P. elliptica* Nutt.). There are ten to fifteen on short stems in a rather loose spike-like raceme. Each flower is about ½ inch (12 mm) across when fully open and appears in July. FRUITS of the greenish-flowered, shinleaf wintergreen and the one-sided, (*P. secunda L.*), species are the round, brown, many-seeded capsules typical of wintergreens. LEAVES are dark green, basal and elliptical, thick, and from 1 to 3 inches (2.5-8 cm) long. Stalks are longer than the leaf blades (in contrast to shinleaf wintergreen in which leaves are borne on shorter stalks). Leaves of the greenish-flowered species are rounded at the ends and are slightly toothed. GROWTH HABIT is perennial, low, 4 to 10 inches (10-25 cm), in which all the height is due to the flower stalks. The illustration of one-sided wintergreen shows the greenish white flowers which all grow to one side of the stem. Common HABITAT of the three species illustrated includes moist areas of deep coniferous woods, particularly pine stands and spruce bogs in the northern and eastern part of the area, but they appear in mixed woods occasionally.

PINESAP
Monotropa hypopithys L.

Pinesap

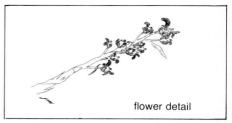

flower detail

Pinesap

FLOWERS are light brown to cream, numerous, urn-shaped, in a rather short, dense raceme. They are hairy, nodding, but erect when mature. There are four or five sepals, which are lance-shaped. Four or five petals closely surround the inner flower parts. Flowers bloom in July. The FRUIT is a many-seeded capsule. LEAVES are scale-like and brown, even more abbreviated than those of Indian-pipe, (*M. uniflora* L.). GROWTH HABIT is saprophytic; stems are light brown and clammy or fleshy. They may rise to 6 to 12 inches (15-30 cm). Common HABITAT is the richer forest soils. It is quite rare but may be found in the Cypress Hills.

INDIAN-PIPE
Monotropa uniflora L.

Indian-pipe

Indian-pipe   flower detail

FLOWERS are waxy white, occasionally with a pinkish tinge, with ten to twelve brownish yellow stamens. They are usually about ¾ inch (2 cm) long with two to four sepals and five petals. They are borne singly and droop until maturity when they move to an upright position. Approximate flowering date is July-August. The FRUIT is an erect many-seeded capsule held in the dried petals and sepals. LEAVES are short, ⅛ inch (3 mm) and appear as white or colorless scales, tipped with black as they mature. GROWTH

HABIT is saprophytic and plants may grow to a height of 12 inches (30 cm) but they are usually nearer 4 inches (10 cm). Stems are nearly translucent and the whole plant has the appearance of a thin rough candle. HABITAT includes deep shade of moist woods, particularly in mature stands of aspen poplar in east and central portions of the area.

PINEDROPS
Pterospora andromedea Nutt.

Pinedrops

Pinedrops

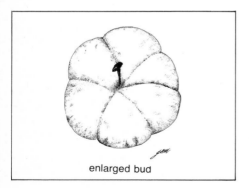

enlarged bud

FLOWERS are brownish cream in color, ¼ to ⅜ inch (6-10 mm) across. They are urn-shaped but much more rounded than those of pinesap, (*Monotropa hypopithys* L.). Flowers are nodding and grow on a long hairy spike, appearing in July. The FRUIT is a yellowish pink many-seeded capsule. LEAVES, more or less basal, are thick, brownish and scale-like. GROWTH HABIT is saprophytic; the stem is thick, coarse, somewhat ribbed, glandular and hairy. The plant grows from a rounded mass of roots and may reach a height of 40 inches, (1 m) of which 25 inches (60 cm) may be the flower spike. HABITAT includes coniferous forest, particularly pine stands. It is found in Saskatchewan in the Cypress Hills and in the foothills region of Alberta.

BOG LAUREL
Kalmia polifolia Wang.

Bog laurel

flower detail

FLOWERS are pink to reddish purple, with five-lobed sepals and five petals in a wheel-shaped corolla. The ten stamens are held in creased pouches in the corolla. Flowers are ⅜ to ¾ inches (1-2 cm) across, borne in clusters in the upper leaf axils. Approximate date of flowering is June. FRUIT is an ovoid capsule about ¼ inch (6 mm) long. LEAVES are opposite, ½ to 1¼ inches (12-30 mm) long on short petioles. They are linear-lanceolate, dark green above and lighter beneath due to fine hairs on the underside. Their edges are usually somewhat rolled. GROWTH HABIT is more or less erect but the stems are weak. These shrubs may attain a height of 3 feet (90 cm) but are more commonly 10 to 12 inches (25-30 cm) tall. Each stem is sharply two-edged and arises from the rootstock. HABITAT includes sphagnum bogs in areas where spruce is dominant. This laurel favors rather sunny open areas, roadsides, etc., more than deep woods. It is known in most of the north and east but is not common. Its leaves are poisonous, particularly to sheep.

Bog laurel

BEARBERRY
Arctostaphylos uva-ursi (L.) Spreng.

Bearberry

FLOWERS are pinkish white, urn-shaped and drooping, in dense terminal racemes. The corolla is four or five-lobed and about 3/16 inches (4 mm) long. Flowering occurs from May-July. FRUIT is a red drupe, ¼ to ⅜ inches (6-10 mm) diameter, which often persists into the next season. It is edible but dry, tasteless and contains five small nutlets. LEAVES are alternate, dark green and more or less evergreen, thick and oblong ovate. The older leaves are orange to reddish brown. The Indians of the plains called it "kinnikinik" and are reputed to have smoked the leaves in their pipes. GROWTH HABIT is prostrate. Trailing stems of this shrub may be 24 inches (60 cm) long and often form a mat on several square yards (meters) of ground. HABITAT includes dry sandy slopes of couleès or the edges of coniferous or mixed woods. It is general throughout the area from the Cypress Hills to the Qu'Appelle Valley and into the boreal forest.

Bearberry

fruit and seeds

LABRADOR TEA
Ledum groenlandicum Oeder

Labrador tea

FLOWERS are white, ¼ inch (6 mm) diameter when open. The five sepals are tooth-like and small and clasp the five spreading petals. The inflorescence is a dense, round-topped umbel at the end of each stem. 'Flowers appear June-July. FRUIT is an oblong, many-seeded capsule, about ¼ inch (6 mm) long with the style persisting at its apex. LEAVES are linear-oblong, dark gray green above and rusty-woolly below, ½ to 2 inches (1-5 cm) long, with strongly rolled margins. They were used as a substitute for tea by early travellers in the Canadian north. GROWTH HABIT is perennial, a branched semi-decumbent shrub from 1 to 4 feet (30-120 cm) tall, with brown bark on rather weak stems. HABITAT includes the boreal forest and its margins across the whole area, extending into the parkland in the valleys of some rivers.

Labrador tea

flowers and leaves

124

CANADA BLUEBERRY
Vaccinium myrtilloides Michx.

leaves and fruit — dwarf bilberry

Canada blueberry

FLOWERS are bell-shaped, greenish white in dense clusters or short racemes. The pinkish white flowers of the dwarf bilberry, (*V. caespitosum* Michx.) are single or fewer than in Canada blueberry. Flowers appear June-July. FRUIT is a sweet tasting blue berry about ¼ inch (6 mm) diameter, with a whitish bloom. LEAVES are alternate, dark green with very short petioles. They are elliptical, ¾ to 1½ inches (2-4 cm) long, (shorter and narrower in dwarf bilberry), and are lighter and slightly hairy on the underside. GROWTH HABIT: A low shrub 12 to 24 inches (30-60 cm) high, usually nearer the former height, with many branches. Dwarf bilberry is shorter, below 12 inches (30 cm) and is inclined to be semi-decumbent. Common HABITAT includes the floor of coniferous forests, particularly under jack pine or in open spaces among them. There are several species which are called blueberries, the commonest being the two described here. In combination they are widely distributed in the boreal forests of the area.

Canada blueberry

SALINE SHOOTINGSTAR
Dodecatheon pauciflorum (Durand) Greene

Saline shootingstar

Mountain shootingstar

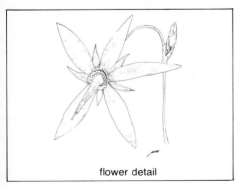

flower detail

Flowers are a striking color combination, produced by the reddish violet reflexed petals and their bright yellow throat or stamen tube. They are borne on a long stem in a terminal cluster which may have as many as twelve flowers. Flowers bloom in June. A mountain species, *D. cylindrocarpum* Rydb., flowers in May, and has fewer blooms. The FRUIT is a five-valved, many-seeded capsule. LEAVES are basal, lance-shaped to spatulate, 1½ to 7 inches (4-17 cm) long, tapering into the petioles. GROWTH HABIT is perennial, from fibrous fleshy roots. The long flower stalks, 4 to 12 inches (10-30 cm), are usually smooth, but are glandular-hairy in some species. HABITAT is moist saline grasslands. It is often found in badly drained meadows near streams. Saline shootingstar is commonest in the south and central part of the area with mountain shootingstar and Cusick's shootingstar, (*D. cusickii* Greene), more common in the southwest.

SEA-MILKWORT
Glaux maritima L.

Sea-milkwort

flowers and leaves

FLOWERS are pinkish cream, but this color is due to the sepals. Petals are lacking and the cup-shaped calyx of five sepals encloses five stamens. Flowers appear in July. The FRUIT is an ovoid capsule 1/16 inch (2 mm) across which contains two to five seeds. It is enclosed by the calyx. LEAVES are opposite, linear to oblong, deep gray green and rather thick. They are stalkless. GROWTH HABIT is low and branching; stems of about 6 inches (15 cm) arise from a creeping rootstock. Numerous leaves per stem give the plant a bushy appearance. HABITAT includes saline meadows and slough margins throughout the area but the plant is not common. Some sites where it grows should be protected.

MEALY PRIMROSE
Primula incana M. E. Jones

Mealy primrose

Mealy primrose

FLOWERS are pale lilac with a conspicuous yellow center. The whole flower is small, ¼ inch (6 mm) diameter. There are five petals, each with a deep notch at its apex. They are borne in an umbel-like cluster on a leafless flower stalk, 4 to 12 inches (10-30 cm) long. Approximate flowering date is June. The FRUIT is a short capsule, often covered by the dried sepals. LEAVES are pale green above and sulphur yellow below. They are arranged in a basal rosette, and are elliptic to ovate, 1 to 2¼ inches (2.5-6 cm) long. GROWTH HABIT is perennial and basal, except for the long flower stalk, which may be up to a foot (30 cm) high. HABITAT includes saline meadows, open moist slopes and slough margins throughout the area. The plant is not plentiful and should therefore not be picked, nor should its habitat be destroyed.

FRINGED LOOSESTRIFE
Lysimachia ciliata L.

Fringed loosestrife

Fringed loosestrife

Tufted loosestrife

FLOWERS are bright yellow, ¾ to 1 inch (2-2.5 cm) in diameter. Petals are irregularly fringed at their tops. They are borne in groups of two or three in the upper leaf axils. Flowers appear in July. FRUIT is an ovoid capsule with five valves. LEAVES are opposite, light green, smooth, 2 to 6 inches (5-15 cm) long, oval to lance-shaped, pointed at the base and rounded at the apex. Petioles are ½ to ¾ inch (12-20 mm) long and have a hairy fringe on one side. GROWTH HABIT is erect, but the stem is weak and plants tend to fall over if not supported by other vegetation. Plant height is usually about 12 inches (30 cm) but some are about 3 feet (1 m). HABITAT includes wooded places, scrubby areas and roadside ditches in any part of the area where moisture is fairly plentiful. Tufted loosestrife, (*L. thrysiflora* L.), may be found in similar or more swampy habitat in the north and east.

OBLONG-LEAVED GENTIAN
Gentiana affinis Griseb.

Oblong-leaved gentian

Northern gentian

Oblong-leaved gentian

FLOWERS are dark blue to purple, usually just over 1 inch (2.5 cm) in length. They are tubular with fringed petals and are borne in a raceme-like cluster of a few flowers at the end of each major stem. Flowers may appear singly. The northern gentian,

(*G. amarella* L.), is somewhat smaller and variable in flower color from purplish blue to greenish yellow and white. Flowers appear August-September. FRUIT is a dry, oblong capsule, composed of two or more valves. LEAVES are opposite, stalkless, light green, oblong to lanceolate, and ½ to 1¼ inches (12-30 mm) long. GROWTH HABIT is erect, perennial, leafy, weak-stemmed and often prostrate, with several stems arising from a deep taproot. Height is usually 4 inches (10 cm) or less but may be nearly 12 inches (30 cm). HABITAT includes moist slough margins, particularly where the soil is sandy, and the moist edges of trees and scrub throughout most of the area, but the plant is most common in the east central portion.

SMALL FRINGED GENTIAN
Gentiana procera Holm

Small fringed gentian

Small fringed gentian

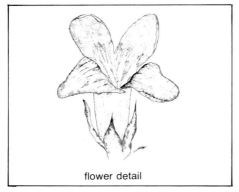

flower detail

FLOWERS are deep sky blue, ¾ to 1¾ inches (2-4.5 cm) long, ½ inch (12 mm) across. Both calyx and corolla are four-lobed and tubular, but the sepals are much shorter than the petals. Lobes of the corolla are fringed. They are borne singly at the ends of stems but the stems occasionally branch near the top. Flowers appear August-September. The FRUIT is an urn-shaped capsule, composed of two or more valves. LEAVES are rather light green, opposite, lanceolate to linear, simple, edges almost rolled, more or less clasping the stem, stalkless and ¾ to 1½ inches (2-4 cm) long. GROWTH HABIT is erect, annual, somewhat leafy, low growing, 4 to 10 inches (10-25 cm) tall. They are usually single stemmed but occasionally branch from the root crown. Some taxonomists separate the fringed gentians into another genus, *Gentianella*. HABITAT is moist ground, particularly near scrub or in open deciduous woods. The small fringed gentian and another species, *G. crinata* Froel., known simply as the fringed gentian, are common in the northern and eastern parts of the area.

BUCK-BEAN
Menyanthes trifoliata L.

Buck-bean

Buck-bean

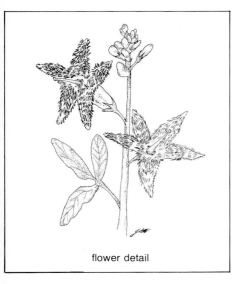

flower detail

FLOWERS are whitish inside, pinkish purple outside, about ½ inch (12 mm) long, with a tube-shaped, five-part corolla, bearded on the inside. They are arranged in a compact raceme at the end of a leafless stalk. Flowers bloom in June. FRUIT is an oval capsule ⅝ inch (15 mm) long, with several long, ⅜ inch (10 mm) seeds in each valve. LEAVES are bright green, elliptical, basal and trifoliate. Each leaflet is 3 to 4 inches (7.5-10 cm) long and the leaves are on long petioles which grow up from the rootstock. GROWTH HABIT is erect, basal in pattern with most stems 4 to 12 inches (10-30 cm) high. HABITAT includes moist and boggy places in marshes, forest bogs and shallow water of ditches. It is common in wooded sections, particularly on the east side of the area.

SPREADING DOGBANE
Apocynum androsaemifolium L.

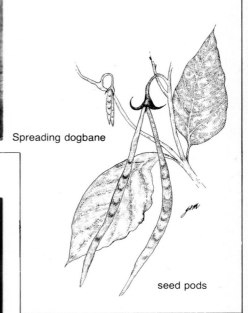

Spreading dogbane

seed pods

Spreading dogbane

FLOWERS are pinkish white, ⅛ inch (3 mm) across, ¼ inch (6 mm) long, bell-shaped with five petals and five sepals. Petals are often streaked with a darker pink and may be reflexed downward. Flowering occurs June-July. FRUITS are pairs of many-seeded pods, 1 to 4 inches (2.5-10 cm) long. LEAVES are opposite, bright green, lighter and somewhat hairy on the underside, ovate to oblong, tipped at the apex, from 1 to 3 inches (2.5-7.5 cm) long. Leaves turn bright yellow or red in the autumn. GROWTH HABIT is perennial, a bushy shrub which grows from a horizontal rootstock. Some bushes may grow to a height of 3 to 4 feet (90-120 cm), but they are usually about 15 inches (40 cm) tall. Its branching and method of spreading makes it a major component of many patches of scrub. HABITAT includes wooded areas of parkland and moister coulees on the prairies, road allowances, etc.

SHOWY MILKWEED
Asclepias speciosa Torr.

Showy milkweed

Showy milkweed

Dwarf milkweed

FLOWERS are pink to pinkish purple, 1/3 to ½ inch (8-12 mm) long, tubular, with the five petals and five sepals both reflexed downwards. Blooms are numerous and arranged in a dense globular umbel which may be 2 to 3 inches (5-7 cm) across. Their strong, sweet smell is said to have a stupefying effect on insects. Flowers bloom in July. FRUIT is a soft many-seeded pod which may be up to 3 inches (8 cm) long and nearly ½ inch (1 cm) thick at the base. The seeds are white-woolly and covered with soft projecting tubercles. LEAVES are dark green, opposite, thick and fleshy. They are oval, 3 to 6 inches (8-15 cm) long, smooth-margined and somewhat heart-shaped at the base. GROWTH HABIT is perennial, up to 6 feet (2 m) tall, often in large clumps. Their size and numerous thick leaves cause some alarm, and while this species is more widely distributed than other species of milkweed, it is no real problem as a weed. When stems and leaves are broken a milky juice oozes out, and it is from this property that the whole genus gets its common name, "milkweed". HABITAT includes scrubby areas at the edges of fields or in pastures, particularly in moist areas in the grasslands and southern aspen parkland. Another species, dwarf milkweed, (*A. ovalifolia* Dcne.), is more common in the upper slopes of the Qu'Appelle Valley and the creeks which drain into it.

HEDGE BINDWEED
Convolvulus sepium L.

Hedge bindweed

Hedge bindweed

Wild morning-glory

FLOWERS are white, faintly streaked with pink, 1½ to 2½ inches (4-7 cm) across, funnel-shaped with the five petals flaring widely at the top. Two large leaf-like bracts enclose the calyx. Field bindweed, (*C. arvensis* L.), is similar but has smaller, distinctly pink flowers. In this species the bracts subtending flowers are smaller and borne well below the calyx. Flowers appear June-August. FRUIT is a capsule which encloses four brownish black angular seeds. LEAVES are light green, alternate, smooth, broadly spear-shaped, 2 to 5 inches (5-13 cm) long and borne on long petioles. GROWTH HABIT is perennial and twining or creeping and stems are weak and slender. It may have stems several feet long which climb over snowberry, chokecherry and other shrubs. HABITAT includes the edges of roads and patches of scrub where moisture conditions are relatively good. It is widely distributed but most common in the Qu'Appelle Valley and its tributaries.

MOSS PHLOX
Phlox hoodii Richards.

Moss phlox

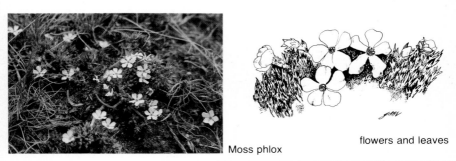

Moss phlox

flowers and leaves

FLOWERS are white to pale violet, ⅜ inch (1 cm) diameter; corolla is a short tube but is distinctly five-lobed. Flowers grow directly attached to the short main stems of the plant and form whitish patches on the ground, appearing in early MAY. FRUIT is a dry capsule enclosed by the five hairy sepals. LEAVES are gray green, ⅛ to ⅜ inch (6-10 mm) long, finely hairy, awl-shaped, closely clasping to the stems. GROWTH HABIT is short and tufted, not much more than an inch (2.5 cm) above the ground.

After the flowers fade the leaves and stem form an inconspicuous part of the ground cover. HABITAT includes the open prairie and dry eroded hillsides of the south and central part of the area. The plant is named for Robert Hood, midshipman on Sir John Franklin's expedition of 1819-22.

NARROW-LEAVED PUCCOON
Lithospermum angustifolium Michx.

Narrow-leaved puccoon

flowers and leaves

FLOWERS are bright lemon yellow with a tube nearly an inch (2.5 cm) long; the face of the flower is ¼ inch (6 mm) in diameter. Petals are distinctly fringed. Flowers are in a terminal cluster of three to four blooms, and appear May-June. FRUIT is four small, white nutlets enclosed in the hairy sepals. LEAVES are gray green, alternate, hairy and ½ to 2 inches (1.5-5 cm) long. GROWTH HABIT is semi-erect or decumbent, with slight branching. Plants grow from a woody taproot to a maximum height of about 8 inches (20 cm). HABITAT is the open prairie where moisture conditions are reasonably good, through the south and southwest of the area, replaced by the hoary puccoon, (*L. canescens* [Michx.] Lehm.), in the east and central portions.

Narrow-leaved puccoon

HOARY PUCCOON

Lithospermum canescens (Michx.) Lehm.

Hoary puccoon

unopened flower

FLOWERS are deep orange to orange yellow, corolla tube ½ inch (1.5 cm) long, and the diameter of the flower is about ¼ inch (6 mm). They are borne in a rather compact leafy cluster at the top of the plant. In moist springs this flower sets pasture fields ablaze. Flowers appear in June. FRUIT is made up of four hard shiny white nutlets. LEAVES are gray green, alternate, stalkless, linear-oblong, ¼ to ½ inch (6-12 mm) long, covered with soft hairs.

GROWTH HABIT is erect; plants may be 6 to 18 inches (15-45 cm) tall, rarely branched. HABITAT includes moist meadows, edges of patches of scrub and aspen poplar, road ditches and railway grades throughout the central, east and northern parts of the area.

Hoary puccoon

TALL LUNGWORT
Mertensia paniculata (Ait.) G. Don

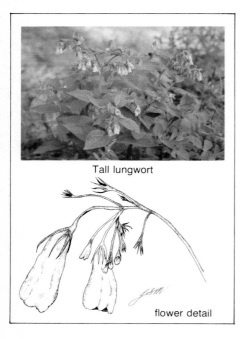

Tall lungwort

flower detail

FLOWERS are bright blue, often with a purplish tinge. The corolla tube is about ½ inch (1-2 cm) long. Drooping clusters of a few flowers are found at the ends of stems. Flowers appear June-July. FRUIT is four small nutlets encased in the five sepals. LEAVES are dark green, alternate, lanceolate, from 2 to 5 inches (5-12 cm) long, slightly hairy on both sides. GROWTH HABIT is tall, 1 to 3 feet (30-90 cm) and much branched. Stems are rather weak and 15 inches (40 cm) is a common height. HABITAT includes moist, shaded areas of aspen poplar groves and mixed forest of the northern parklands. The plant is plentiful and a pleasant sight in shady areas and on stream banks. Other species are also known in the area.

Tall lungwort

CLUSTERED OREOCARYA
Oreocarya glomerata (Pursh) Greene

Clustered oreocarya

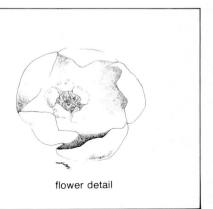

flower detail

FLOWERS are white with yellow centers, ⅜ inch (1 cm) across, each with a short, tubular corolla. They are arranged in compact clusters at the ends of stems and appear in June. FRUIT is composed of four triangular nutlets which are encased in the enlarged sepals. LEAVES are grayish green due to short bristly hairs on their surface. Lower leaves are spatulate, 1 to 2 inches (2.5-5 cm) long and upper leaves are shorter and linear. GROWTH HABIT is erect, 2 to 12 inches (5-30 cm) high with a group of several hairy, branching stems growing from a woody root. HABITAT includes dry open areas on the southern grasslands, but the plant is often found in crevices in rocks or on roadsides. It is occasionally referred to as "miner's candle".

Clustered oreocarya

GIANT-HYSSOP
Agastache foeniculum (Pursh) Ktze.

Giant-hyssop

Giant-hyssop

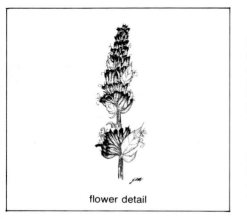

flower detail

FLOWERS are blue, ¼ to ⅜ inches (6-10 mm) across, borne in a dense spike. The spike may lack flowers for a short space and its total length may be 3 to 4 inches (7.5-10 cm). The corolla is tubular and two-lipped and the four stamens protrude. Approximate flowering date is July-August. FRUIT is made up of four small nutlets held in the cup-shaped calyx. LEAVES are opposite, dark green above and paler on the lower surface, 1 to 3 inches (2.5-7.5 cm) long. They have short petioles, are coarsely-toothed and pointed at the apex. GROWTH HABIT is tall, erect and branching on rather weak square stems, 1 to 3 feet (30-90 cm) in height. Plants have a pleasant anise-like odor. HABITAT includes the edges of aspen poplar groves and thickets in the parkland and prairie.

WILD MINT
Mentha arvensis L.

Wild mint

Wild mint

flower detail

FLOWERS are bluish, occasionally with a purple tinge, about ⅛ inch (3 mm) long with a tubular calyx and four or five-lobed tubular corolla. As with many mints there are only four stamens. The flowers appear in crowded whorls at several of the upper leaf axils, July-August. FRUIT is four small oval nutlets, held in the tube formed by the sepals. LEAVES are opposite, bright green and rough. They are oval to lanceolate, pointed at the apex, ½ to 1½ inches (1-4 cm) long, almost hairless, with minute glandular dots on both surfaces. GROWTH HABIT is erect, perennial, on light green square stems, 4 to 18 inches (10-45 cm) tall. The stem and leaves have a pleasant mint smell when crushed and are occasionally used as flavoring. HABITAT includes grassy sloughs and moist places, particularly in the central, north and east of the area. The plant may grow in water but usually does not.

WESTERN WILD BERGAMOT
Monarda fistulosa L.

Western wild bergamot   seed head

FLOWERS are pink or lilac and occasionally white with a typical two-lipped corolla. They are fuzzy, ¾ to 1½ inches (2-4 cm) long, numerous in a globose head-like cluster, 1 to 1½ inches (2.5-4 cm) across when in full bloom. The calyx of each flower forms a narrow green tube, ½ inch (12 mm) long with purplish teeth, and the combination of these tubes forms the head. Flowers bloom July-August. FRUIT is composed of four small nutlets. LEAVES are opposite, gray green due to fine hairs, triangular-ovate on short petioles and pointed at the apex, 1 to 3 inches (2.5-7.5 cm) long. GROWTH HABIT is perennial and erect on stiff square stems which do not often branch. Leaves, stems and flower heads have a strong pleasant odor. HABITAT includes the edges of scrubby patches and aspen poplar groves and various moist waste places throughout the area. A variety, (*menthaefolia* [Graham] Fern.), with shorter leaf stalks and hairy leaves is more common, particularly in the west.

Western wild bergamot

MARSH SKULLCAP
Scutellaria epilobiifolia Hamilton

Marsh skullcap

Marsh skullcap

flower detail

FLOWERS are deep blue, ⅜ to ¾ inch (1-2 cm) long with a tubular calyx and a two-lipped corolla typical of the mints. A single flower or a pair develops in upper leaf axils and there are usually not more than two flowering groups per plant. Appearance of flowers is June-August. FRUIT is four small, tough nutlets held tightly in the calyx. LEAVES are opposite, bright green, oblong to lanceolate, wavy-margined, 1 to 2½ inches (2.5-7 cm) long. The lower ones are short stalked and the upper ones stalkless. GROWTH HABIT is perennial, erect but short, usually under 10 inches (25 cm), on slender square stems. HABITAT includes wet saline meadows and other wet places around sloughts and ditches, particularly in the parkland and the parkland-prairie transition area. These flowers are a pleasant find in long grass in upper levels of marshes.

MARSH HEDGE-NETTLE
Stachys palustris L.

Marsh hedge-nettle

Marsh hedge-nettle

bud stage

FLOWERS are pale purple to white with dark purple spots, ⅜ to 1 inch (1-2.5 cm) long. The calyx is funnel-shaped. The corolla is two-lipped but the upper lip is more erect than in other mints and the lower more distinctly three-lobed. The flowers are found in spike-like axillary clusters near the top of the plant, July-August. FRUIT is four small nutlets held in the tube of the dried calyx. LEAVES are opposite, light green, coarsely toothed and hairy, lance-shaped to oblong, stalkless or on short petioles. They are generally rounded at the base. GROWTH HABIT is perennial, erect, occasionally branching, arising from creeping rhizomes. The stem is coarse, hairy and square and the height is usually about 12 inches (30 cm) but may reach up to 4 feet (120 cm). HABITAT includes marsh edges and roadside ditches throughout the area, particularly in the east and central section.

LARGE WHITE GROUND-CHERRY
Physalis grandiflora Hook.

Large white ground-cherry

Black henbane

Wild tomato

FLOWERS are white with a pale yellow center, wheel-shaped and somewhat bell-shaped too, 1¼ to 1½ inches (3-4 cm) in diameter, borne in the upper leaf axils. Flowers appear in July. FRUIT is a green berry partly enclosed in a persistent calyx, 1 inch (2.5 cm) long, and about ⅜ inch (1 cm) in diameter. LEAVES are dark green, prominently veined, ovate to lanceolate, 1½ inches (4 cm) long, smooth margined, somewhat sticky, borne on petioles 1 to 2 inches (2.5-5 cm) long. GROWTH HABIT is annual, erect from creeping rootstocks, but stems tend to flop over due to the weight of leaf growth. Stems are somewhat hairy and sticky. HABITAT is the floor of heavy woods in the north and east. The prairie ground-cherry, (*P. virginiana* Mill.), is more common on sandy prairies to the south. Fruits and flower parts of all three plants illustrated on this page warrant care and caution. They are dangerous poisons. The other members of the same plant family illustrated are the wild tomato, (*Solanum triflorum* Nutt.), and the black henbane, (*Hyoscyamus niger* L.).

SCARLET PAINTBRUSH
Castilleja coccinea (L.) Spreng.

Scarlet paintbrush

Red Indian paintbrush

Lance-leaved paintbrush

FLOWERS are noticeable due to the colored bracts which surround them. The bracts are red in this species and yellow, cream or deep red in others. Actual flowers are within the bracts in a dense terminal spike. Flowers are yellow green and tubular. The corolla is two-lipped with a large upper lip (galea) and a three-lobed lower lip, about ¾ to 1 inch (2-2.5 cm) long, barely visible among the bracts. Note the differences in color in the two other species illustrated; red Indian paintbrush, (*C. mineata* Dougl.), and lance-leaved paintbrush, (*C. acuminata* [Pursh] Spreng.). Approximate flowering date is July. FRUIT is a dry, many-seeded capsule about ¾ inch (2 cm) long. LEAVES are alternate, simple, occasionally lobed and stalkless. They are 1 to 2 inches (2.5-5 cm) long, linear and pointed. GROWTH HABIT is usually perennial, leafy, 12 to 24 inches (30-60 cm) high. The plant is sometimes parasitic upon plant roots. HABITAT includes the margins of aspen groves, roadsides and patches of larger shrubs over most of the parkland. Scarlet paintbrush is the commonest of the species shown. The lance-leaved species is more common on open hillsides and edges of patches of scrub in the southeast and red Indian paintbrush is found in the Cypress Hills.

TOAD-FLAX
Linaria vulgaris Mill.

Toad-flax

Toad-flax

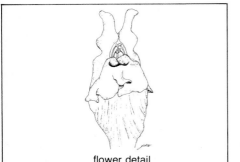

flower detail

FLOWERS are bright yellow with orange throats and have long spurs at the base. There are five sepals and five petals, and the corolla is distinctly two-lipped. Flowers are 1 to 1¼ inches (2.5-3 cm) long, arranged in a dense terminal raceme and appear June-July. FRUIT is an oval capsule, ⅜ to ⅝ inches (1-1.5 cm) long which contains several flattened seeds, each of which has a circular wing. LEAVES are alternate, gray green, linear and stalkless, ¾ to 3 inches (2-7.5 cm) long. Another species, (*L. dalmatica* [L.] Mill.), has an ovate to lanceolate leaf which clasps the stem. GROWTH HABIT is perennial, arising from creeping rootstocks. The stems, 8 to 24 inches (20-60 cm) tall, are somewhat branched and rather slender. HABITAT is variable but the plant is common in abandoned gardens, railway yards, roadside ditches, etc. Both species were introduced as garden plants.

YELLOW MONKEYFLOWER
Mimulus guttatus DC.

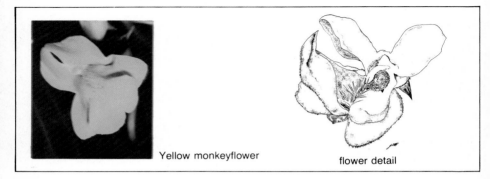

Yellow monkeyflower

flower detail

FLOWERS are deep yellow, usually spotted with red, and hairy in the ridges of petals. They are ¾ to 1¼ inches (2-3 cm) long, with four stamens in pairs. The corolla is two-lipped. Flowers are borne singly or in a short raceme on rather slender stalks. Two other species are known in the prairie provinces, one with blue flowers and one with red flowers. Flowers bloom in July. The FRUIT is a two-valved, many-seeded capsule. LEAVES are opposite, medium green, ovate or rounded, ½ to 2 inches (1-5 cm) long, lower leaves stalked and upper leaves usually clasping the stem. GROWTH HABIT is perennial, plants arising in branches from a common base 8 to 24 inches (20-60 cm) in height. Stems are erect but slender and often trail on other plants. HABITAT includes shady areas along the banks of running streams in the west of the area, and particularly in the Cypress Hills.

Yellow monkeyflower

LILAC-FLOWERED BEARDTONGUE
Pentstemon gracilis Nutt.

White beardtongue

flower detail—
Lilac-flowered beardtongue

FLOWERS are pale lilac, with a tubular corolla of five petals about ¾ inch (2 cm) long. The five sepals are deeply separated but the calyx is distinctly tubular. A white species, (*P. albidus* Nutt.), is also shown. Flowers appear June-July. FRUIT is the dry many-seeded capsule typical of the beardtongues. LEAVES are opposite, gray green, more or less smooth, linear-oblong to lanceolate and slightly toothed, 1 to 3 inches (2.5-7.5 cm) long. GROWTH HABIT is erect and perennial on smooth slender stems usually 6 to 18 inches (15-45 cm) high. The white species and slender beardtongue are both somewhat shorter. HABITAT includes moist grasslands and slough margins, particularly in the south and central part of the area.

Lilac-flowered beardtongue

SMOOTH BLUE BEARDTONGUE
Pentstemon nitidus Dougl.

Smooth blue beardtongue

Slender beardtongue

flower detail —
Smooth blue beardtongue

FLOWERS are bright blue with a slight lavender tinge, arranged in a spike-like raceme. The tubular corolla is about ¾ inch (2 cm) long, distinctly two-lipped and open. The lower lip is bearded with fine smooth hairs. Stamens are separated and one of the five stamens is bearded and sterile. Flowering occurs May-June. FRUIT is a dry, many-seeded capsule. LEAVES are opposite, gray green due to a velvety bloom on their surface, oval to lance-shaped, smooth-margined, 1 to 2 inches (2.5-5 cm) long. GROWTH HABIT is erect, usually branched, 4 to 12 inches (10-30 cm) high. Stems are hairless. HABITAT includes the dry eroded hillsides and river brakes of the grasslands and the plant is often found in sandy soils and under rather poor moisture conditions. Another distinctly blue species is slender beardtongue, (*P. procerus* Dougl.).

WESTERN BUTTERWORT
Pinguicula macroceras Willd.

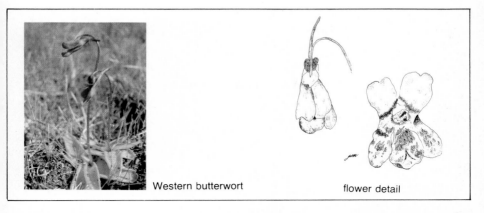

Western butterwort   flower detail

FLOWERS are deep purple, up to ¼ inch (6 mm) across, with a straight spur about ¼ inch (6 mm) long. The spur is curved in the other native species, (*P. vulgaris* L.). Petals are somewhat hairy, particularly near the mouth of the tube. Flowers appear in June. FRUIT is a two-valved capsule. LEAVES are basal, pale yellowish green, ¾ to 1½ inches (2-4 cm) long, ¾ inch (2 cm) wide, sticky. The edges are somewhat rolled and have shallow teeth. GROWTH HABIT is characterized by basal leaves and an erect flower stem 2 to 5 inches (5-13 cm) in length. Common HABITAT includes the edges of water runs and saline meadows of the Cypress Hills and a few other places in the southern portion of the area. It is replaced by *P. vulgaris* to the north and east. This plant is rare; do not pick it or dig it up.

Western butterwort

COMMON BLADDERWORT
Utricularia vulgaris L.

Common bladderwort

Common bladderwort

flower detail

FLOWERS are deep yellow, ½ to ¾ inch (1-2 cm) long, stalked and widely spaced on a leafless spike. The corolla is two-lipped and has a short spur. Flowers appear in June. The FRUIT is a many-seeded capsule divided into two valves. LEAVES are brownish green, finely-divided and numerous, ¾ to 2 inches (2-5 cm) long. They bear numerous bladders which float the plant near the surface of the water. GROWTH HABIT is aquatic and stems and leaves combine to make a mat of plants near the surface so that flowers may be raised above the water. HABITAT includes most of the prairie sloughs of the whole area, where the striking yellow of bladderwort is a pleasant sight to the road-weary traveller.

NORTHERN BEDSTRAW
Galium boreale L.

Northern bedstraw

Sweet-scented bedstraw

Northern bedstraw

FLOWERS are white, ⅛ inch (3 mm) diameter with no sepals and a distinctly four-lobed wheel-shaped corolla. The pistil has two styles. Approximate flowering date is July-August. FRUIT is a pair of rounded nutlets, 1/16 inch (1 mm) long and densely covered with whitish hairs. LEAVES are bright green, arranged in whorls of four. They are linear, three-ribbed and pointed, 1 to 2 inches (2.5-5 cm) long. GROWTH HABIT is perennial and erect on slender square stems from thin brown rootstocks, 8 to 24 inches (20-60 cm) tall. The sweet-scented species, (*G. triflorum* Michx.), is a finer-stemmed plant, much more trailing in habit. HABITAT includes the aspen poplar groves and associated scrub of the parkland region to where parkland and forest meet. Sweet-scented bedstraw is more common in the boreal forest.

TWINING HONEYSUCKLE
Lonicera glaucescens Rydb.

Twining honeysuckle

Twining honeysuckle

Twining honeysuckle

FLOWERS are yellow, turning red as they age, tubular, ¾ to 1 inch (2-2.5 cm) long, held at the stem tip in a whorled leaf. Flowers appear July-August. The FRUIT is a round berry, bright red when ripe. LEAVES are light green, opposite, often joined at the bases, and joined to form the whorled leaf at the base of the flower cluster. The margins are smooth. GROWTH HABIT: A woody shrub, more or less twining, often attaining a height of 6 feet (180 cm) or more, but usually under 3 feet (90 cm). Common HABITAT includes edges of aspen poplar groves or shady roadsides where it twines on other shrubs. It is found throughout the parkland area and in occasional coulees in the prairie area.

TWINFLOWER
Linnaea borealis L.

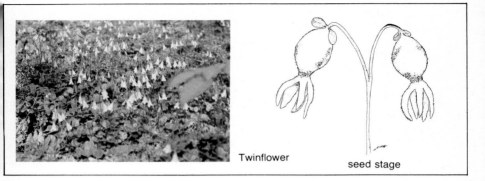

Twinflower

seed stage

FLOWERS are pinkish white, ⅛ inch (3 mm) across, bell-shaped, paired and nodding from a stem about 4 inches (10 cm) long. These flower stalks are numerous along the creeping stem. Approximate flowering date is June-July. FRUIT is an oval, hairy, one-seeded capsule. LEAVES are opposite, oval, short-stalked, somewhat wavy-margined, ⅜ to ⅝ inch (1-1.5 cm) wide. GROWTH HABIT is creeping and evergreen. Stems may be up to 30 inches (75 cm) long. HABITAT includes open and semi-shaded areas of mixed woods and coniferous woods, particularly in the north and east. It is named for Linnaeus, founder of our system of taxonomic botany.

Twinflower

WESTERN SNOWBERRY
Symphoricarpos occidentalis Hook.

Western snowberry

Thin-leaved snowberry

Western snowberry

FLOWERS are pink and white, about ¼ inch (6 mm) long, with several tubular five-lobed flowers in a dense terminal or axillary cluster. Stamens and pistil project above the corolla in western snowberry but not in thin-leaved snowberry, (*S. albus* [L.] Blake). Flowers appear in July. FRUIT is a waxy white berry which later dries to a light brown. LEAVES are opposite, gray green, ovate to oval, somewhat hairy on the underside, 1 to 3 inches (2.5-7.5 cm) long. In the thin-leaved snowberry the leaves are usually slightly toothed. GROWTH HABIT is perennial, a low bushy shrub, 1 to 4 feet (30-120 cm) high with hollow stems. They grown in dense clumps from creeping rootstocks. Common HABITAT includes the ravines and low spots of the open prairie and the margins of patches of chokecherries and other shrubs throughout the area. It is commonly known as "buckbrush."

HIGH BUSH-CRANBERRY
Viburnum trilobum Marsh

High bush-cranberry

High bush-cranberry

Low bush-cranberry

FLOWERS are white in the sterile florets to creamy white in the fertile florets, with five petals, five sepals and five stamens. The outer sterile flowers are ½ to ¾ inch (12-20 mm) across and have five large petals. The whole flower cluster may be 2 to 6 inches (5-15 cm) across. Both sterile and fertile florets are present in each cluster. Flowers appear in June. FRUIT is a red berry, tart and edible, nearly a ¼ inch (6 mm) in diameter with a large flat seed. LEAVES are opposite, deeply three-lobed, 2 to 4 inches (5-10 cm) wide, coarsely and irregularly toothed. They are palmately-veined, deep green above and lighter beneath. GROWTH HABIT: A tall shrub with a few smooth, reddish gray branches, 3 to 12 feet (1-4 m) in height. In another species, the low bush-cranberry, (*V. edule* [Michx.] Raf.), the plant reaches about 4 feet (120 cm) and has many slender branches. HABITAT includes open areas in aspen poplar groves or scrubby areas of the parkland, river valleys and low places. The low bush-cranberry is more frequent in moister, heavily-wooded areas. Neither of these species should be confused with *Vaccinium oxycoccus* L. and *Vaccinium vitis-idaea* L. which are known as cranberry, but are of the same genus as the blueberries.

HAREBELL
Campanula rotundifolia L.

Harebell   flower and bud

FLOWERS are bell-shaped, blue of varying depth, this color increasing with the intensity of the shade in their location. They are ⅝ to ¾ inch (1.5-2 cm) long and about ⅜ inch (1 cm) diameter, often borne singly but sometimes in a loose raceme. Flowers bloom June-September. FRUIT is a papery, many-seeded capsule. LEAVES are linear to linear-oblong, ½ to 3 inches (1-7.5 cm) long. Basal leaves appear at an early stage of growth, are about 1 inch (2.5 cm) long, ovate and heart-shaped at the base. GROWTH HABIT is perennial and erect. Height may vary from 4 to 18 inches (10-45 cm). HABITAT includes the meadows, cultivated hayfields and roadsides throughout the area, even to the edge of the boreal forest.

Harebell

WILD CUCUMBER
Echinocystis lobata (Michx.) T. and G.

Wild cucumber   dry fruit

FLOWERS are greenish white and unisexual. Male flowers are in panicles or racemes and the female flowers, on the same plant, are less plentiful and located in the axils of leaves. Flowers appear in June. FRUIT is a large, ovoid, fleshy berry, 1 to 1½ inches (2.5-4 cm) long, known as a pepo, with a thick, pale green skin. It is covered with long weak spines. Each fruit contains several large flat, roughened dark brown to black seeds. LEAVES are alternate, thin, pale green, palmately veined, rough on both sides, 2 to 5 inches (5-12.5 cm) across, deeply divided into five to seven large lobes. GROWTH HABIT is annual. The stem is twining, 10 to 20 feet (3-6 m) long and somewhat angled. Twining is aided by frequent long, spirally-twisted tendrils. Vines twine through bushes 3 to 5 feet (90-150 cm) above the ground. HABITAT includes moist places along creeks and rivers in the southeast and south central parts of the area.

Wild cucumber

KALM'S LOBELIA
Lobelia kalmii L.

Kalm's lobelia

Spiked lobelia

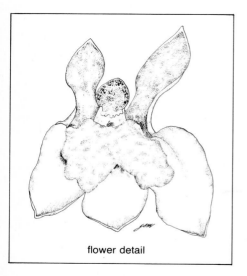

flower detail

FLOWERS are light blue, fading to white on the inside near the base, ⅜ inch (1 cm) long. Each flower has two wing petals above and three below and they are borne in a loose raceme of a few flowers. The corolla is split to separate the lower lip from the upper three petals. The spiked lobelia, (*L. spicata* Lam. var. *hirtella* A. Gray), is also shown. Flowers appear in July. FRUIT is a short pod-like capsule. LEAVES are alternate, spatulate on the lower stem and linear above, ½ to 1 inch (12-24 mm) long, bluish green and numerous. They are borne on short petioles. GROWTH HABIT is biennial or perennial, 4 to 12 inches (10-30 cm) high on a slender branching stem. Common HABITAT includes bogs, wet meadows and road ditches through the central parklands; the plant is frequently found in calcareous soils.

LARGE-FLOWERED FALSE DANDELION
Agoseris glauca (Pursh) Raf.

Large-flowered false dandelion

Common dandelion

Large-flowered false dandelion

FLOWERS are deep orange yellow, made up of ray florets only. Flowers are usually about 1 inch (2.5 cm) in diameter but may be nearly 2 inches (5 cm). The flower stem is 8 to 15 inches (20-40 cm) high and there is usually one flower per plant. The common dandelion, (*Taraxacum officinale* Weber), is shown for contrast. Flowers bloom July-August. FRUIT is a dry, beaked achene with a white pappus. LEAVES are bluish green, usually basal, narrowly lanceolate, sometimes with a few teeth, usually about 3 to 5 inches (7-12 cm) long but may be up to 10 inches (25 cm). GROWTH HABIT is perennial, with basal leaves in a dense rosette and a long flower stalk of up to 15 inches (40 cm). HABITAT: Widely distributed over the prairie and to the edges of the parkland in moister grassy areas, roadside ditches, etc.

NARROW-LEAVED HAWK'S-BEARD
Crepis tectorum L.

Narrow-leaved hawk's-beard

flowers and seed heads

FLOWERS are deep yellow, in heads up to ½ inch (12 mm) in diameter, composed of ray florets only. They are ringed with short bracts and grow on branched stalks, July-September. FRUIT is an achene, 3/16 inch (4 mm), with a reddish brown seed, slight beak and white pappus. LEAVES are dark green, oblanceolate to spatulate and often slightly toothed with backward-pointing teeth. Basal leaves may be up to 6 inches (15 cm) long but stem leaves are shorter and distinctly linear, 1½ to 3 inches (4-8 cm) long. GROWTH HABIT is annual or occasionally perennial, from a thick, branched root supporting a dense mat of leaves and the tall flower stalks. Stems exude a milky juice when broken. They may be hairy or smooth and vary in height from 8 to 36 inches (20-90 cm). Hawk's beard species are easily confused with the hawkweeds, (*Hieracium* spp. [Tourn.] L.). Hawkweeds have a distinctly brown pappus on their seeds and are fibrous rooted. HABITAT includes edges of moist meadows, field edges and margins of aspen poplar groves or patches of scrub.

Narrow-leaved hawk's-beard

BLUE LETTUCE
Lactuca pulchella (Pursh) DC.

Blue lettuce

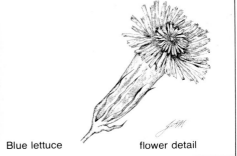

Blue lettuce   flower detail

FLOWERS are bright powdery blue, up to an inch (2.5 cm) across, with ray florets only, borne in a loose panicle of three to five blooms, August-September. FRUIT is a dry achene with a small white pappus. LEAVES are alternate, pale bluish green, with a distinct bloom, linear-lanceolate, often with lobes that point backward toward the stem. They may be up to 7 inches (18 cm) long. GROWTH HABIT is perennial with tall slightly-branched stems growing from running rootstocks. Stems and roots exude a milky sap when broken. Plant height varies from 15 to 36 inches (40-90 cm). HABITAT includes the margins of roads, gravel pits and fields where the soil is fairly heavy and moist, although the ground where this plant grows usually appears rather inhospitable. It is common throughout Saskatchewan but more common in the southern third.

GLAUCOUS WHITE-LETTUCE
Prenanthes racemosa Michx.

Glaucous white-lettuce

Glaucous white-lettuce

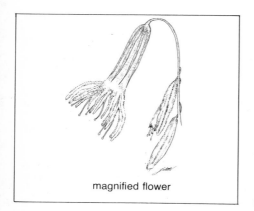

magnified flower

FLOWERS are greenish or yellowish white, ½ to ¾ inch (12-20 mm) diameter, disc-shaped, composed of ray florets only. They are slightly scented and borne in drooping heads in a long terminal panicle. Heads are enclosed in a group of linear purplish bracts. Flowers appear in August. FRUIT is an elongated ribbed achene with a pale cinnamon brown pappus. LEAVES are alternate and mainly stalkless, 1 to 2 inches (2.5-5 cm) long, up to an inch (2.5 cm) wide. The lower leaves may be stalked and are triangular or heart-shaped. The upper leaves are lance-shaped. GROWTH HABIT is perennial; the smooth erect stem may be 2 to 5 feet (60-150 cm) tall, but it is usually nearer 2 feet (60 cm). Stems exude a milky sap when broken. HABITAT includes the open areas in aspen poplar groves in the northeast and central portions of the area.

PERENNIAL SOW-THISTLE
Sonchus arvensis L.

Perennial sow-thistle

Annual sow-thistle

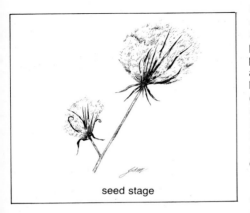

seed stage

FLOWERS are deep yellow, ½ to 1¼ inches (1-3 cm) in diameter. Only ray florets are present. Several flower heads are ar-ranged in a rounded panicle, and appear June-September. FRUIT is a dry, flattened achene with a white pappus. The seeds produced per plant are a major factor in the problem of this plant as a weed. LEAVES are bluish green with backward pointing lobes and prickly margins, 4 to 10 inches (10-25 cm) long. The upper leaves are stalkless, less lobed and shorter; the lower leaves have short petioles. GROWTH HABIT is perennial in this species and annual in the other species shown, (*S. oleraceus* L.). Stems exude a milky sap when broken. They have few branches and leaves are mostly basal. Height of plants varies from 1 to 5 feet (30-150 cm). HABITAT includes gardens, roadsides and weedy fields throughout the area. It is sometimes a significant source of pollen and nectar for honeybees.

GOAT'S-BEARD
Tragopogon dubius Scop.

Goat's-beard

Goat's-beard

FLOWERS are yellow with only ray florets and the outer ones are wider. Blooms may be 1½ to 2 inches (3.5-5 cm) across. All flowers are complete as far as sex structures are concerned. Beneath the ray florets are ten to fourteen green, pointed involucral bracts which are longer than the outer ray florets. Approximate flowering date is July-August. The FRUIT is a narrow, beaked achene, 1 to 1¼ inches (2.5-3.5 cm) long, with a plume-like pappus. The whole fruiting head is a striking sight. LEAVES are erect and grass-like, 4 to 12 inches (10-30 cm) long and under ½ inch (1 cm) wide. They are stalkless and clasp the stem. GROWTH HABIT is biennial, stems are coarse, up to ⅝ inch (1.5 cm) diameter, 6 to 24 inches (15-60 cm) high, from a fleshy taproot. They contain a milky sap. Flowers appear at ends of stems and stems are thickened below the flower head. HABITAT includes yards, roadsides, railway grades and waste land; the plant is more common on prairies than parkland. This species was probably introduced from western United States. Another species, meadow goat's-beard, (*T. pratensis* L.), is similar but smaller and flowers are chrome yellow with shorter bracts.

Goat's-beard

YARROW
Achillea millefolium L.

Many-flowered yarrow

seed stage —
Yarrow

Yarrow

FLOWERS are usually white, but occasionally light pink. Color is mainly due to the sterile ray florets. The ten to thirty disc florets are yellow to light cream. Involucral bracts overlap in three or four rows. The flower heads are 1½ inches (4 cm) across and are densely packed in a round topped terminal cluster. The many-flowered yarrow, (*A. sibirica* Ledeb.), has flowers in a flat topped cluster. Flowers appear June-August. FRUIT is a small flattened dry achene with no pappus. LEAVES are woolly, blue green, 1½ to 6 inches (4-15 cm) long, 1 inch (2.5 cm) wide, divided into many segments. Leaves average 3 inches (7.5 cm) long. The leaves of many-flowered yarrow are linear and deeply toothed but not in segments, and somewhat less hairy. GROWTH HABIT is perennial, with several stems arising from a branched rootstock. Stems are not much branched and are very woolly-hairy. HABITAT includes roadsides and open prairie throughout the area with the other species more common at the edges of aspen poplar groves in the north and east. Yarrow is one of the commonest white flowers of the summer scene in Saskatchewan.

LOW EVERLASTING
Antennaria aprica Greene

Low everlasting

Rosy everlasting

Prairie everlasting

FLOWERS are white to cream color, occasionally slightly pink, in heads ¼ to ½ inch (7-12 mm) tall. Ray florets are absent; disc florets are creamy white and have either stamens or pistil, (sometimes both sexes are on the same plant). Bracts are thin, white, or translucent and overlap the flower heads. Several flower heads are present in each compact cluster which is so shaped that the flower is often called "pussy toes." Flowering date ranges from June-July. The FRUIT is a dry achene with a white pappus. LEAVES are woolly white on both sides and form a close mat on the ground. Individual leaves are spatulate or wedge-shaped, ⅜ to ¾ inch (1-2 cm) long. Stem leaves, if present, are ⅜ inch (1 cm) long and linear. The prairie everlasting, (*A. campestris* Rydb.), has yellowish green leaves which are almost devoid of hairs on the upper surface. GROWTH HABIT is basal, and even with the flower stems, plants are rarely over 6 inches (15 cm) tall in low everlasting as well as in rosy everlasting, (*A. rosea* Greene). However one species, the showy everlasting (*A. pulcherrima* [Hook.] Greene), may grow to 20 inches (50 cm). HABITAT includes dry prairie or dry meadows of the parkland in the case of the low and prairie everlasting. About a dozen species are known for the area and one, (*A. dimorpha* Nutt.), is rare and worthy of serious protection.

HEART-LEAVED ARNICA
Arnica cordifolia Hook.

Heart-leaved arnica

Shining arnica

Heart-leaved arnica

FLOWERS are deep orange yellow due to many wide ray florets and the closely-grouped disc florets. Each stem usually has a single flower head, 1 to 2 inches (2.5-5 cm) diameter, June-July. The FRUIT is a dry hairy achene with a barbed, white to creamy pappus. LEAVES on the stem are heart-shaped, opposite, usually stalkless and bright green and smooth, 1 to 3 inches (2.5-7 cm) long. They are distinctly smaller and less lobed than the basal leaves. Another species is referred to as shining arnica, (*A. fulgens* Pursh), and has smaller, linear-lanceolate leaves. GROWTH HABIT is perennial and erect, with leaves growing along the coarse stem which may be 8 to 24 inches (20-60 cm) tall. HABITAT includes the reasonably moist soils and slough edges in grassy areas where the plants may not be noticed until flowers open. Both species are common in the south and southwest. The heart-leaved arnica is more common in the west and in the Cypress Hills.

SMOOTH ASTER
Aster laevis L.

Smooth aster

Lindley's aster

Showy aster

FLOWERS are bright violet blue due to their ray florets; disc florets are dark yellow. The heads, about ¾ inch (2 cm) across, are borne in a loose panicle and each head has a circle of green-tipped bracts loosely grouped beneath it. Also illustrated are two other asters of similar flower color, Lindley's aster, (*A. ciliolatus* Lindl.), and showy aster, (*A. conspicuus* Lindl.).

Lindley's aster is deeper blue than the other two. Flowers appear August-September. The FRUIT is a ribbed, flattened achene with numerous pappus bristles. LEAVES are alternate, dark green, thick and smooth-surfaced, usually somewhat toothed, ovate to lanceolate. Basal leaves have wide-margined stalks and upper leaves are stalkless and often clasping. Lindley's aster has conspicuously-winged petioles. GROWTH HABIT is usually perennial and erect but "flopping." Height varies from 1 to 4 feet (30-120 cm), usually nearer the former. Stems are more or less smooth. HABITAT includes the wooded areas of the parkland, scrubby roadside ditches and some moist open places on the prairie. Lindley's aster is more common in open spaces among trees than the smooth aster.

MANY-FLOWERED ASTER
Aster pansus (Blake) Cronq.

Many-flowered aster

Willow aster

seed stage — White prairie aster

FLOWERS have white ray florets and yellow disc florets. The flower heads are relatively small, ⅜ inch (1 cm) diameter but very numerous. They are mostly found on one side of the curved stems, where 4 to 7 inches (10-17 cm) of the end of each stem may bear flowers. Bracts are arranged in three series around the heads. Flowers appear August-September. FRUIT is an achene with distinct ridges and a pappus with hairs of variable length. LEAVES are alternate, gray green, narrow, linear, ½ to ¾ inch (12-20 mm) long with smooth margins. They are quite numerous. Leaves of the willow aster, (*A. hesperius* A. Gray), are much longer, up to 6 inches (15 cm) and occasionally slightly toothed. GROWTH HABIT: A cluster of several wiry hairy stems arising from a thick tufted rootstock to a height of 8 to 24 inches (20-60 cm). The willow aster is more branched and much taller, up to 40 inches (1 m). HABITAT includes grassy edges of fields, open meadows and edges of scrubby patches. The plant is common throughout the area, but more common on the open prairie than the willow aster. The white prairie aster, (*A. falcatus* Lindl.), is also illustrated (seed stage).

NODDING BEGGARTICKS
Bidens cernua L.

Nodding beggarticks

flower detail

FLOWERS are usually nodding, ¾ to 1¼ inches (2-3 cm) in diameter, deep yellow in color, with the center darker or speckled yellow and black. The outer bracts are nearly 1 inch (2.5 cm) long and slightly reflexed, and are slightly longer than the ray florets. Approximate flowering date is August-September. FRUIT is a spear-shaped achene, about ¼ inch (6 mm) long with four barbed awns which are backward pointing. LEAVES are dark green, opposite, somewhat paler on the underside, stalkless and clasping, 2 to 6 inches (5-15 cm) long, toothed and linear lanceolate. GROWTH HABIT is annual, erect and leafy on coarse, angled stems, height 24 to 30 inches (60-75 cm). HABITAT includes wet slough edges and the margins of sloughs which have recently dried up, particularly in the eastern part of the area.

Nodding beggarticks

NODDING-THISTLE
Carduus nutans L.

Nodding-thistle

Nodding-thistle

Russian-thistle

FLOWERS are deep purple, borne in single heads, 1 to 2 inches (2.5-5 cm) in diameter. The heads are on nodding, angled, spineless stems, 8 to 10 inches (20-25 cm) in length. Involucral bracts are in many series, purple at maturity and possessing a prominent mid-vein that develops into a spine. Flowers appear July-August. FRUIT is a smooth, spotted, brown achene, about ¼ inch (6 mm) long, with a white pappus that lacks a plume. LEAVES are alternate, deeply divided, gray green, well covered with spines and clasping the stem. GROWTH HABIT is biennial, branching and tall, 3 to 5 feet, (90-150 cm) with many flower heads per plant. The stem is angular and somewhat ridged. HABITAT includes roadside ditches, fence edges, field borders, etc., particularly in the central part of the area. Nodding-thistle was introduced and is not the same genus as the native thistles. The third illustration shows another introduction, Russian-thistle, (*Salsola pestifer* A. Nels.).

HAIRY GOLDEN-ASTER
Chrysopsis villosa (Pursh) Nutt.

Hairy golden-aster

Hairy golden-aster

seed stage

FLOWERS are bright yellow due to the ray florets while tubular florets range from orange to brown. There may be one or several flower heads, 1 to 1¼ inches (2.5-3 cm) across, present at the ends of each branch, July-September. FRUIT is a flattened hairy achene. The pappus is double on each fruit. LEAVES are alternate, gray green due to their hairiness, oblong to lanceolate, 1 to 2 inches (2.5-5 cm) long and numerous. They are usually short-stalked or stalkless. GROWTH HABIT is bushy, with branches arising from a woody taproot. Branches are often nearly prostrate but some plants reach a height of 24 inches (60 cm). HABITAT includes dry sandy prairie and hillsides, particularly in the south and south-central part of the area.

CANADA THISTLE
Cirsium arvense (L.) Scop.

Canada thistle

Canada thistle

Wavy-leaved thistle

FLOWERS are lavender blue to purple and occasionally white. All florets are disc or tubular type and all florets on a plant are of the same sex. The florets are arranged in loose corymbose heads at the ends of stems. The male heads are up to 1 inch (2.5 cm) across and the female heads nearer ½ inch (12 mm). In the wavy-leaved thistle, (*C. undulatum* [Nutt.] Spreng.), flowers are purple to pink and are larger: 2 inches (5 cm) across and solitary at ends of branches. Flowers bloom July-September. FRUIT is a small, flat, smooth achene with a white pappus. LEAVES are alternate, dark green, stalkless, sometimes clasping. They are lanceolate, curled or wavy and deeply incised into spined segments. In the wavy-leaved thistle the lower leaves are stalked. GROWTH HABIT is perennial, growing to 1 to 3 feet (30-90 cm) from deep running rootstocks. It often appears in patches and is rather slender. HABITAT includes road-sides and cultivated fields where moisture conditions are fairly good. The wavy-leaved thistle is more common in the south and west.

SHORT-STEMMED THISTLE
Cirsium drummondii T. and G.

Short-stemmed thistle   bud detail

FLOWERS are unusual because of their large size, with heads up to 2 inches (5 cm) across and equally tall. They are deep rose purple and the center head usually matures first with up to five lesser heads blooming around it later. The other species illustrated is Flodman's thistle, (*C. flodmanii* [Rydb.] Arthur), which has flowers of similar color but somewhat smaller heads, 1 to 1½ inch (2.5-4 cm) across. Flowers appear in July. The FRUIT is a flat achene, 3 to 5 mm long with a creamy white bristly pappus. LEAVES appear basal due to the shortness of the stem; they are smooth and green on both sides when mature, stalkless, 3 to 6 inches (8-15 cm) long, triangular-lobed with weak spines. GROWTH HABIT is perennial, low and squatty, 4 to 12 inches (10-30 cm) tall, usually nearer the lower figure. Flodman's thistle is much taller, up to 36 inches (90 cm). HABITAT includes the eastern and north eastern portions of the area (Togo and Parr Hill Lake); the plant is usually found in grassy meadows in woods. Flodman's thistle is common across the prairies and parkland throughout the area.

Flodman's thistle

COMMON TICKSEED
Coreopsis tinctoria Nutt.

Common tickseed

Common tickseed

seeds

FLOWERS have deep orange yellow ray florets and reddish brown disc florets. They are usually about an inch (2.5 cm) across and borne on long, slender, smooth stems. The ray florets are broad, three-lobed at the apex, and may be tinged with purple at the base. Flowers bloom August-September. FRUIT is an achene that lacks a pappus and is curved so that it distinctly resembles a tick or small insect. LEAVES are mainly opposite, stalkless or nearly so, 2 to 4 inches (5-10 cm) long, once or twice divided into linear or lanceolate lobes. Upper leaves are less divided than the lower ones and lower leaves are more often stalked. GROWTH HABIT is erect and annual, stems are slender, hairless and much branched, usually about 12 inches (30 cm) tall but may be as tall as 36 inches (90 cm). HABITAT includes moist places in road ditches and edges of grassy marshes in rather sandy soil. The wild species may be noticed particularly because of the flowers' deep orange color and dark center. Other species are hardy garden annuals.

TUFTED FLEABANE
Erigeron caespitosus Nutt.

Tufted fleabane

Daisy fleabane

bud and flowers — Tufted fleabane

FLOWERS are white with a yellow center, 1 inch (2.5 cm) in diameter and often appear singly. Ray florets are numerous, (60-90), and about ⅜ inch (1 cm) long. Each head is surrounded by three or four series of bracts thickened at the back. Daisy fleabane, (*E. strigosus* Muhl.), is similar but bracts are not thickened and ray florets are more numerous. Flowers appear in July. FRUIT is a dry achene with a bristly pappus, typical of the fleabanes. LEAVES are gray green, smooth-margined and three-veined. Basal leaves are oblong-lanceolate, 1 to 3 inches (2.5-7 cm) long and have petioles, but upper leaves lack petioles, are reduced in size and linear oblong in shape. GROWTH HABIT is, as the name implies, tufted, with several curving stems, 6 to 12 inches (15-30 cm) tall from a thick root crown. HABITAT includes dry prairie and hillsides of the south and central part of the area.

SMOOTH FLEABANE
Erigeron glabellus Nutt.

Smooth fleabane

Smooth fleabane

Philadelphia fleabane

FLOWERS have purple (occasionally nearly white) ray florets which are ¼ to ⅝ inch (8-15 mm) long and numerous (125-175). Disc florets are yellow with stamens and pistil. Flower heads have linear bracts, ¼ inch (6 mm) long, with a conspicuous brown mid-vein. There may be one to five heads on each plant and each is about ½ inch (12 mm) diameter. Flowers appear June-August. FRUIT is a dry achene with a bristly double pappus. LEAVES are mostly basal, 2 to 4 inches (5-10 cm) long, oblong-lanceolate and hairless. Upper leaves are alternate, toothed, much smaller and linear-lanceolate, with a single prominent vein. The basal leaves of the smooth fleabane have petioles but all the leaves of the Philadelphia fleabane, (*E. philadelphicus* L.), are clasping at the base and spatulate in shape. GROWTH HABIT is perennial, occasionally biennial, with simple or slightly branched stems arising 6 to 18 inches (15-45 cm) from tufted fibrous roots. HABITAT includes the open prairie and edges of scrubby patches through the moister parts, particularly in the north, central and east. The Philadelphia fleabane occupies the same type of habitat, usually in areas that are even more moist than where smooth fleabane grows.

GAILLARDIA
Gaillardia aristata Pursh

Gaillardia

single floret

FLOWER heads are up to 4 inches (10 cm) across with yellow orange ray florets toothed at the apex and set in a rounded brownish purple disc. The ray florets are often purple at the base. Flowers appear July-August. FRUIT is a dry hairy achene with a scaly pappus. LEAVES are alternate, grayish green and hairy, with lower leaves stalked and spatulate; upper leaves are stalkless and smaller than the lower ones, which may be 2 to 5 inches (5-12 cm) long. Upper leaves may be slightly lobed. GROWTH HABIT is erect, a slightly branched, hairy stemmed perennial growing from a slender taproot, usually 8 to 24 inches (20-60 cm) tall. HABITAT includes roadsides, railway grades and drier uplands as far up as the forest edge.

Gaillardia

GUMWEED
Grindelia squarrosa (Pursh) Dunal

Gumweed   flower detail!

Gumweed

FLOWERS are bright yellow, due to both ray and disc florets and are somewhat wheel-like. The heads are ¾ to 1¼ inches (2-3 cm) across and develop on the ends of the plant's many branches. The plant gets its name from the rows of sticky bracts which cover the involucre. Flowers appear July-September. FRUIT is a four or five-ribbed achene with a pappus of two or more awns. LEAVES are alternate, dark green, smooth and glistening. They are oblong-lanceolate, stiff and dotted with glands. The lower leaves have petioles but the upper ones are clasping. The edges have teeth of varying size and are pointed at the apex. GROWTH HABIT is much branched and stems arise from a deep taproot. Plants grow 8 to 24 inches (20-60 cm) high, usually nearer the former. HABITAT includes roadsides, saline flats and slough margins, particularly where there has been overgrazing. The plant is very common in the prairie section and encroaches into the parkland in some places.

BROOMWEED
Gutierrezia diversifolia Greene

Broomweed

Broomweed

magnified flowers

FLOWERS are deep yellow, about ⅛ inch (3 mm) high, 1/16 inch (1 mm) across, in close clusters at the ends of branches. The few ray florets have no stamens; the disc florets have both stamens and pistil. There are usually five or six ray florets and eight to ten disc florets, giving the cluster the appearance of a head of deep yellow, tubular flowers. Approximate flowering date is June-August. FRUIT is a dry, five-angled achene with a scaly pappus. LEAVES are gray green, narrow-linear, 1/16 inch (1 mm) wide, stalkless, and lack marginal indentations. GROWTH HABIT is biennial or perennial, more or less erect on many slender brittle stems which grow from a woody taproot. HABITAT is the dry prairies of the southern third of the area.

RHOMBIC-LEAVED SUNFLOWER
Helianthus laetiflorus Pers. var. subrhomboideus (Rydb.) Fern.

Narrow-leaved sunflower

FLOWERS are yellow heads 1 to 3 inches (2.5-7 cm) across with reddish purple or brownish disc florets. Ray florets vary from ⅝ to 1½ inches (1.5-4 cm) in length. Flower heads are often solitary and appear August-September. FRUIT is a dry achene with the pappus reduced to two awn-like scales. LEAVES are dark green, usually opposite and with the rhombic shape for which it is named. They have three distinct veins and are 2 to 4 inches (5-10 cm) long. GROWTH HABIT is perennial from a thick branching rootstock. The long stem of the single flower is easily noticed and the stems appear bare of leaves and slightly hairy. The narrow-leaved sunflower, (*H. maximilianii* Schrad.), appears even less leafy and the leaves are much narrower and somewhat folded. HABITAT characteristically includes roadsides and field margins. The rhombic-leaved species is more common in dry areas on light soils than the other sunflowers.

Rhombic-leaved sunflower

Rhombic-leaved sunflower

PRAIRIE SUNFLOWER
Helianthus petiolaris Nutt.

Prairie sunflower

Prairie sunflower

seed head

FLOWERS have bright yellow ray florets and yellow brown disc florets, 1 to 3½ inches (2.5-9 cm) across. The scales between the disc florets each have a small tuft of hairs. Approximate date of flowering is July-August. FRUIT is a smooth, dry, slightly ribbed achene which contains a single seed. LEAVES are alternate, deep green and entire margined. They are rough on both surfaces, 1 to 3 inches (2.5-8 cm) long, ovate to lanceolate, with long stalks. GROWTH HABIT is annual, 1 to 3 feet (30-90 cm) tall with some branching of the stem. HABITAT includes roadsides and other disturbed places, particularly where the soil is sandy. The showy sunflower, (*H. lenticularis* Dougl.), will displace it on heavier soils.

COLORADO RUBBERWEED
Hymenoxys richardsonii (Hook.) Cockerell

Colorado rubberweed

Colorado rubberweed

FLOWERS are bright yellow, due to both ray and disc florets. The few ray florets are about ½ inch (12 mm) long and lack stamens. The disc florets have both stamens and pistil. The flower heads are borne at the ends of branches in a flat-topped cluster about ¾ inch (2 cm) across. An illustration of spiny iron plant, (*Haplopappus spinulosus* [Pursh] DC.), is also shown. It flowers in August, about a month later than the Colorado rubberweed. Approximate date of flowering is June-July. FRUIT is an achene and the pappus is short-awned. LEAVES are alternate, dark green, mostly basal, divided into narrow linear lobes up to 1½ inches (4 cm) in length. GROWTH HABIT is perennial, stems rise to 12 inches (30 cm) from a coarse woody taproot which appears as a woolly crown full of dead leaves. The plant is more or less tufted and stems are slightly straggling and slightly hairy. HABITAT includes overgrazed pastures and roadside ditches under rather indifferent moisture conditions throughout the prairies of the area.

Spiny iron plant

DOTTED BLAZINGSTAR

Liatris punctata Hook.

Dotted blazingstar

Dotted blazingstar   Meadow blazingstar

FLOWERS are deep rosy purple, up to ½ inch (12 mm) diameter, with the heads arranged in a dense crowded spike of disc florets. Each head contains four to six tubular florets with plumose pappus hairs among them. The meadow blazingstar, (*L. ligulistylis* [A. Nels.] K. Schum.), has a round head about 1 inch (2.5 cm) diameter and a "shingling" of purplish bracts around it. Flowers appear in August. FRUIT is a ribbed, hairy achene, ¼ inch (6 mm) long with a bristly pappus. LEAVES are bright green with a whitish midvein, stiff and linear, 2 to 6 inches (5-15 cm) long, usually nearer the former. Lower leaves are wider and almost lanceolate. GROWTH HABIT is perennial in a clump of stems which may be somewhat decumbent, but up to 18 inches (45 cm) tall. The stems arise from a thick corm-like rootstock. HABITAT includes open grassy meadows and hillsides in the prairie area, with meadow blazingstar much more common in moister areas, particularly through the parkland-prairie.

WILD CHAMOMILE
Matricaria chamomilla L.

Wild chamomile

Pineapple weed

Ox-eye daisy

FLOWERS have wide white ray florets with yellow disc florets in a center about ½ inch (12 mm) diameter. Ray florets may be up to 1 inch (2.5 cm) and are pistillate. Flower heads are numerous at the ends of branches, July-August. FRUIT is a small (under 1/16 inch or 1 mm) dry achene with three to five faint ribs and no pappus. LEAVES are alternate, light green, stalkless ¾ to 3 inches (2-7.5 cm) long, divided into many threadlike segments. Both leaves and flowers have a pineapple odor when crushed. In contrast, leaves of the ox-eye daisy, (*Chrysanthemum leucanthemum* L.), are broader and spatula-shaped, with toothed margins. They have no odor. GROWTH HABIT is annual, erect and much branched, 6 to 30 inches (15-75 cm) high. Some of the slender stems on taller plants droop somewhat. HABITAT includes roadsides, field margins and meadows, particularly where moisture conditions are good. Another member of the same genus, pineapple weed, (*M. matricarioides* [Less.] Porter), is shown also. It is more widely distributed and frequently appears in yards, gardens and at the edges of walks.

ARROW-LEAVED COLT'S-FOOT
Petasites sagittatus (Pursh) A. Gray

Arrow-leaved colt's-foot

Arrow-leaved colt's-foot

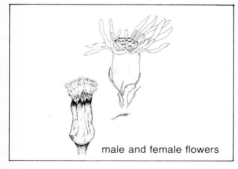

male and female flowers

FLOWERS are white, minute, in dense terminal clusters, either male or female, and sexes are usually on separate plants. The bracts which surround the cluster are in a single series and scaly in appearance. Flowers appear before leaves, May-June. The FRUIT is a dry achene, 3/16 inch (4 mm) long with a white pappus, an unusual sight in the lush green of mid-June. LEAVES are light grayish green above and dense white-woolly beneath, borne on long stems which arise from the root crown. They are triangular-ovate with short marginal teeth. The palmate-leaved colt's-foot, (*P. palmatus* [Ait.] A. Gray), is very similar except for the shape of the leaf, which the common name describes. GROWTH HABIT is perennial; the thick coarse flower stem rises from the root crown to 8 to 30 inches (20-75 cm). This soon dies back and the flannel-like leaves develop. HABITAT includes edges of water-filled ditches and sloughs as well as marshy areas, deep in aspen poplar groves throughout the forest and parkland areas.

PRAIRIE CONEFLOWER
Ratibida columnifera (Nutt.) Woot. and Standl.

Prairie coneflower

Brown coneflower

Purple coneflower

FLOWERS have bright yellow ray florets which are usually reflexed. The receptacle (disc) is columnar, ½ to 1½ inches (1-4 cm) high. The disc florets are yellowish brown and bear both stamens and pistil. Another form, (forma *pulcherrima* [D.C.] Fern.), has purplish brown ray florets but it is quite rare. Ray florets in either are ½ to 1¼ inch (1-3 cm) long and up to ¼ inch (6 mm) wide. Flowers appear July-September. FRUIT is a grayish black, flattened achene, 1/16 inch (2 mm) long, with the pappus reduced to a few scales and one or two small teeth. Leaves are alternate, gray green, pinnately divided and somewhat hairy, 2 to 4 inches (5-10 cm) long. Basal leaves are often not divided. GROWTH HABIT is perennial, erect, stems are hairy and somewhat grooved longitudinally, 10 to 24 inches (25-60 cm) high, with the flower stems ac-counting for at least a third of this height. HABITAT is dry prairie, roadsides, railway grades, etc., of the south and west, being replaced by the black-eyed susan, (*Rudbeckia serotina* Nutt.), to the east and north. Another similar plant illustrated on this page is the purple coneflower, (*Echinacea angustifolia* DC.), which is very rare in Saskatchewan.

BLACK-EYED SUSAN
Rudbeckia serotina Nutt.

Black-eyed susan

Black-eyed susan

flower profile

FLOWERS have ten to twenty striking orange yellow ray florets which are not reflexed. They enclose a dense, flattened, dark brown disc of complete florets. The disc is ½ to 1 inch (1.5-2.5 cm) across and the ray florets are often 1 to 1½ inches (2.5-4 cm) long. Flowers appear July-September. FRUIT is a smooth four-angled achene. LEAVES are medium green, hairy, lanceolate to oblanceolate in the western forms, more oval in the eastern one, (*R. hirta* L.). GROWTH HABIT is biennial, 12 to 18 inches (30-45 cm) tall and hairy, with stem occasionally purplish in color. Leaf stalks account for a third or half the total height. HABITAT includes the edges of aspen poplar groves and scrubby patches or open meadows in the parkland where moisture conditions are good.

MARSH RAGWORT
Senecio palustris (L.) Hook.

Marsh ragwort

FLOWERS are bright, rather pale yellow in ½ to ¾ inch (12-20 mm) heads crowded into a dense terminal cluster which may be somewhat nodding. Flowers appear June-July. FRUIT is a small, dry achene with a white pappus. The seed heads form a woolly cluster and may be present while some flower heads are still blooming. LEAVES are coarse, light gray, 2 to 6 inches (5-15 cm) long, the lower ones with winged stalks and wavy margins, lanceolate to spatulate in shape. The upper ones are somewhat smaller, lobed, stalkless, clasping and linear lanceolate. GROWTH HABIT is annual, with a coarse, hairy, angled, hollow stem, 6 to 24 inches (15-60 cm) high. Stems may be cobwebby when young but soon lose this cover. HABITAT: The immediate margins of prairie and parkland sloughs and lakes across the area; in some years it practically forms a yellow ring around them. The other member of the genus illustrated is silvery groundsel, (S. *canus* Hook.), which is from 12 to 36 inches (30-90 cm) tall with mainly basal leaves.

Marsh ragwort

Silvery groundsel

LOW GOLDENROD
Solidago missouriensis Nutt.

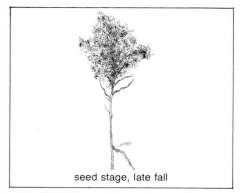

seed stage, late fall

FLOWERS are deep yellow with ten to twenty heads in a rather rounded compact terminal panicle 2 to 3 inches (5-7 cm) long. The individual heads are ⅛ to 3/16 inch (3-5 mm) high and are supported by blunt linear bracts. In contrast, mountain golden-rod, (*S. decumbens* Greene var. *oreophila* [Rydb.] Fern.), blooms later and has the flower heads separated on the upper stem in a longer, narrower panicle. Flowers appear July-August. FRUIT is a small hairy achene with a creamy white pappus. LEAVES are deep green, some basal, some alternate on the stem, and triple veined. Basal leaves are oblanceolate and stalked, 1 to 4 inches (2.5-10 cm) long, but the upper ones are smaller, mostly stalkless and lanceolate to linear. In mountain goldenrod leaves are wider, thicker and more rounded at the tip. GROWTH HABIT is erect and perennial, 4 to 15 inches (5-45 cm) tall. The stems are hairless and usually somewhat reddish. HABITAT includes the dry prairie and hillsides of the south and southwest where it is the first goldenrod to herald the autumn.

Low goldenrod

Mountain goldenrod

VELVETY GOLDENROD
Solidago mollis Bartl.

Canada goldenrod

FLOWERS are bright deep yellow. The heads are dense in a pyramid-like panicle in both velvety goldenrod and Canada goldenrod, (*S. canadensis* L.). The bracts, in several series, are yellowish and somewhat thick and pointed. The whole inflorescence may be 4 inches (10 cm) high and 1½ inches (4 cm) across. The stiff or rigid goldenrod, (*S. rigida* L.), with which velvety goldenrod is often confused, has flower heads in a flat topped inflorescence. Flowers appear August-September. The FRUIT is a small dry achene with a rather bristly pappus. LEAVES are alternate, pale green, oval and stalked. The upper leaves are elliptic and stalkless with three distinct veins. They are covered with short, fine, velvety hairs. Leaves are larger and smooth in Canada goldenrod. GROWTH HABIT is perennial, erect, on stems which tend to be solitary and arise from a horizontal rootstock. Height varies from 8 to 18 inches (20-45 cm). The Canada goldenrod is taller, up to 24 to 30 inches (60-75 cm). HABITAT principally includes the prairie and roadsides of the south and central part of the area. The three species illustrated are probably the commonest of the goldenrods and the most widely distributed. Canada goldenrod is more common in the eastern part.

Velvety goldenrod

Stiff goldenrod

LOW TOWNSENDIA
Townsendia sericea Hook.

Low townsendia

FLOWERS are white to cream, ⅜ inch (1 cm) long, occasionally tinged with pink or light blue due to the ray florets. The conspicuous yellow center is due to disc florets. The flower heads, ½ to 1¼ inches (12-30 mm) are borne on very short stalks and the involucral bracts are flattened to the head and partly overlapping. Approximate flowering date is May-June. The FRUIT is a dry achene with a pappus of forked or barbed hairs. LEAVES are alternate or basal, narrowly spatulate to linear, 1 to 2 inches (2.5-5 cm) long, pale gray due to fine hairs. They have deeply cleft, divided margins. GROWTH HABIT: A low perennial rarely over 1½ inches (4 cm) high, on a short stem which grows from a woody root. HABITAT includes sunny slopes of dry hills of the south and southeast. It appears along with moss phlox, leafy musineon, and other flowers of early spring.

Low townsendia

Townsendia (pink form)

GLOSSARY

ACHENE	A one-seeded, one-celled, dry, hard fruit that does not open when ripe
AWN	A bristle-like part of the inflorescence
AXIL	The upper angle formed where a leaf stalk or a branch joins a stem
AXILLARY	In an axil
BARB	A short, stiff point or short bristle
BERRY	A pulpy fruit with several seeds
BLOOM	The whitish, powdery covering of some fruits
BRACT	A small leaf or scale, often borne below a flower or flower cluster
CALCAREOUS	Pertaining to soil high in calcium salts
CALYX	The outer floral ring or sepals
CAPSULE	A dry fruit consisting of more than one chamber
CARPEL	A seed-bearing chamber at the base of the pistil of a flower
CATKIN	A tight, scaly cluster of flowers of one sex, in which the flowers usually lack petals
CLEFT	Refers to deeply lobed leaves (Fig. 8)
CORM	A thick enlarged base of a plant stem
COROLLA	The petals or inner floral ring
CORYMB	A flower cluster with a flat or rounded top in which flower stalks arise from different points on the stem. (Fig. 3)
CRETACEOUS	The last geological period of marine type rock deposition in Saskatchewan
CYME	A loose flower cluster in which the central flowers open first (Fig. 3)
DECIDUOUS	Trees with leaves that are dropped yearly, not evergreen
DECUMBENT	A stem with the base on or near the ground, with tip or main stem erect
DICOTYLEDON	A plant with two cotyledons or seed leaves
DIOECIOUS	Having the flowers with pistils or with stamens on separate plants
DISCOID	Having only disc flowers
DRUPE	A pulpy or fleshy fruit containing a single seed enclosed in a hard shell or stone
ENTIRE	Refers to a leaf, having a margin not toothed or cleft
FLORET	A single flower, usually of a composite head or cluster
FOLLICLE	A fruit with a single chamber that opens along one side
GLABROUS	Leaves or stems which lack hairs, i.e., smooth
GLANDULAR	Bearing secreting organs or glands
GLAUCOUS	Covered with a bloom
GLOBOSE	Spherical or nearly so

GLOBULAR	Globe-like
GRANULAR	Covered with very small grainy structures
HIP	The berry-like, enlarged calyx tube of roses, containing many achenes
INFLORESCENCE	The arrangement of groups of flowers on a plant (Fig. 3)
INTERNODE	The part of a stem between two nodes
INVOLUCRE	The whorl of bracts below a flower cluster
KEEL	The two lower united petals of flowers of legumes
LANCEOLATE	Narrow leaves, broadest at the base and tapering to the tip. (Fig. 7)
LIGULE	A strap-shaped organ, as in ray florets of Compositae
LINEAR	Leaves, long and narrow, with parallel margins (Fig. 7)
LIP	The main lobe of a two-lobed corolla or calyx, particularly in the orchid family
LOBE	A rounded projection of a leaf or a leaf-like part of a plant
LOCULE	One of the compartments of a pistil or anther
LOMENT	A pod in which there are constrictions between the seeds
MONOCOTYLEDON	A plant with only one cotyledon or seed leaf
MONOECIOUS	Having pistils and stamens in separate flowers on the same plant
NODE	The place on a stem where leaves grow or normally arise
OBLANCEOLATE	Leaves of a shape longer than broad and tapering to the tip (Fig. 7)
OBOVATE	Leaves of an egg shape with the broader end towards the tip (Fig. 7)
OVAL	Leaves of an egg shape with ends equally tapered (Fig. 7)
OVARY	The part of the pistil of a flower containing the cells that become seeds
OVATE	Leaves of an egg shape broader towards the petiole (Fig. 7)
OVOID	Egg-shaped with the wide part near the point of attachment
PALMATE	A simple or compound leaf divided into finger-like parts or leaflets (Fig. 8)
PANICLE	A flower cluster in which the lower branches are longer (Fig. 3)
PAPPUS	The bristly or scale-like appendage on fruits of Compositae
PETAL	A separate part of the corolla or inner floral ring, usually brightly colored (Fig. 4)
PETIOLE	The stalk of a leaf
PINNATE	Refers to compound leaves with leaflets on each side of the stalk (Fig. 8)
PISTIL	The central ovule-bearing organ of a flower, made up of stigma, style and ovary
PLUMOSE	Having fine hairs
POD	A dry fruit, opening when mature
POME	A fleshy fruit
PUBESCENT	Leaves or stems which are covered with fine hairs
RACEME	A flower cluster with each flower borne on a short stalk arising at different points on a common stem (Fig. 3)
RECEPTACLE	The end of the flower stem bearing flower parts
REFLEXED	Bent sharply backwards, as with sepals or petals
RHIZOME	An underground, root-like stem
SAPROPHYTIC	Living on dead organic matter
SCAPE	A flowering stem growing from the root crown and not bearing proper leaves

SCURFY	Refers to leaves and stems, covered with small scale-like particles
SEPAL	One of the separate parts of a calyx, usually green and leaf-like (Fig. 4)
SPADIX	A dense or fleshy spike of flowers
SPATHE	A large leaf-like bract enclosing a flower cluster
SPATULATE	Leaves which are spoon-shaped with a broad, rounded tip, tapering to the petiole (Fig. 7)
SPIKE	A flower cluster with stalkless individual flowers on a common stalk (Fig. 3)
SPUR	A hollow projection, usually at the base of a flower
STAMEN	The pollen-bearing part of a flower consisting of anther and filament
STIGMA	The upper part of the pistil where the pollen is received
STIPULE	An appendage at the base of a leaf
STYLE	The part of the pistil joining the stamen and ovary
TAXONOMY	The study and practice of classification of organisms
TRIFOLIATE	Three leaves attached to a common petiole (Fig. 8)
TUBERCLE	A rounded protruding body attached to some part of a plant
UMBEL	A flower cluster in which all flower stalks arise from one point (Fig. 3)
WHORL	A group of three or more leaves arising from the same node (Fig. 2)
WOOLLY	Covered with tangled soft hairs

BIBLIOGRAPHY

Bailey, L. H. *Manual of Cultivated Plants Most Commonly Grown in the United States and Canada.* Rev. ed. New York: Macmillan Co., 1949.

Boivin, Bernard. *Flora of the Prairie Provinces: A Handbook to the Flora of the Provinces of Manitoba, Saskatchewan and Alberta.* Reprinted from *Phytologia,* 15-23 (1967-1972).

Breitung, August J. *Annotated Catalogue of the Vascular Flora of Saskatchewan.* Reprinted from *American Midland Naturalist,* 58 (1957).

Britton, Nathaniel Lord, and Addison Brown. *An Illustrated Flora of the Northern United States and Canada,* 1-3 (1913). 2d ed. New York: Dover Publications, 1970.

Budd, A. C. and J. B. Campbell. "Flowering Sequence of a Local Flora," *Journal of Range Management,* 12 (1959): 127-132.

Budd, Archibald C. and Keith F. Best. *Wild Plants of the Canadian Prairies.* Publication 983. Ottawa: Canada Department of Agriculture, 1964.

Canada Weed Committee. *Common and Botanical Names of Weeds in Canada.* Publication 1397. Ottawa: Canada Department of Agriculture, 1975.

Carmichael, Lloyd T. *Prairie Wildflowers.* Toronto: J. M. Dent and Sons (Canada) Limited, 1961.

Cormack, R. G. H. *Wild Flowers of Alberta.* Edmonton: Alberta Department of Industry and Development, 1967.

Moss, E. H. *Flora of Alberta: A Manual of Flowering Plants, Ferns and Fern Allies Found Growing Without Cultivation in the Province of Alberta, Canada.* Toronto: University of Toronto Press, 1959.

Scoggan, H. J. *Flora of Manitoba.* National Museum of Canada Bulletin No. 140. Biological Series No. 47. Ottawa: Canada Department of Northern Affairs and Natural Resources, 1957.

INDEX

Common and Scientific Names

INDEX

Plant Families

COLOR INDEX TO PLANTS *

Red - Pink

*This index classifies plants according to four main color groups: white, purple-blue, red-pink and greenish-yellow-cream. Some plants may appear in more than one color group. — Eᴅ.

Purple - Blue

White

Greenish - Yellow - Cream

PHOTO CREDITS

Fenton R. Vance is the primary photographer for *Wildflowers Across the Prairies*. An alphabetical listing of the names of contributing photographers follows, indicating the pages on which each may be found:

D. E. ANDREWS 91 (bottom left); V. ANDREWS 31 (bottom), 142 (top left), 153 (top left); W. C. BLIGHT 30 (top), 62 (top left), 91 (top), 108 (top right); G. J. BUCK 119 (top); L. T. CARMICHAEL 39 (bottom), 47 (top), 111 (top), 112 (top left), 175 (bottom right), 179 (bottom left and bottom right), 182 (top right), 183 (top left), 185 (middle and bottom); W. B. CLIPSHAM 135 (bottom left); C. W. CUTHBERT 123 (bottom left); D. GILROY 36 (top left), 141 (top), 150 (top right); D. R. M. HATCH 9 (top), 121 (top left), 131 (top left), 161 (bottom right), 172 (bottom); A. C. HUME 56 (top left), 61 (middle left), 126 (top), 173 (bottom left); J. R. JOWSEY 17 (top left), 30 (bottom left), 53 (bottom left), 56 (bottom right), 122 (bottom right), 164 (top left); S. I. JOWSEY 186 (top); F. W. LAHRMAN 13 (top), 14 (top right), 19 (bottom), 55 (top left), 83 (top right), 116 (top left), 124 (bottom), 139 (bottom), 145 (bottom right), 148 (bottom), 151 (bottom), 163 (bottom left); J. H. MACDONALD 123 (top), 144 (bottom left); R. W. MOFFATT 146 (bottom right), 194 (bottom right); L. A. MORGOTCH 43 (top left); J. L. PARKER 152 (bottom left); K. M. PATTERSON 108 (top left), 193 (top left); C. B. PRATT 106 (bottom left), 119 (bottom left), 138 (top left), 164 (top right), 176 (top left), T. B. RIFFEL 36 (bottom), 87 (top left and bottom), 114 (top), 165 (top right); S. D. RIOME 154 (top), 187 (bottom right); L. R. SCOTT 137 (bottom); G. W. SEIB 16 (top left), 17 (bottom), 23 (top left), 25 (bottom left), 26 (bottom), 37 (top left), 49 (bottom left), 59 (top left and top right), 64 (top), 82 (bottom left), 90 (top left and top right), 98 (top left), 102 (middle left), 104 (bottom), 108 (bottom left), 110 (top right), 156 (top right), 168 (bottom right), 185 (top left); A. H. SHORTT 27 (bottom left), 115 (top left), 130 (top right); J. E. SLOUGH 66 (bottom left), 79 (bottom left), 106 (top); O. STILL 165 (top left); S. STRETTEN 189 (bottom right); F. A. SWITZER 28 (top), 32 (bottom), 51 (bottom left), 52 (top left), 54 (top), 57 (top), 70 (bottom), 72 (top), 83 (top left), 89 (bottom left), 105 (bottom left), 107 (top left), 117 (top right), 127 (top and bottom left), 128 (top left), 130 (top left), 131 (top right), 141 (bottom left), 143 (bottom left), 146 (top), 147 (top right), 155 (bottom), 160 (top right), 174 (top), 178 (top), 184 (top right), 192 (bottom left); C. F. TRIMMER 94 (bottom); S. M. VAN BRIENEN 65 (bottom right).